Positive Parenting

Positive Parenting

Raising Children with Self-Esteem

Elizabeth Hartley-Brewer

VERMILION
LONDON

10 9 8 7 6 5 4

First published in the United Kingdom in 1994 by Mandarin Paperbacks

Re-issued in 1998 by Vermilion, an imprint of
Ebury Press
Random House UK Ltd
Random House
20 Vauxhall Bridge Road
London SW1V 2SA

Random House Australia (Pty) Ltd
20 Alfred Street
Milsons Point Sydney
New South Wales 2061 Australia

Random House New Zealand Limited
18 Poland Road, Glenfield
Auckland 10 New Zealand

Random House South Africa (Pty) Limited
Endulini, 5A Jubilee Road
Parktown 2193, South Africa

Random House UK Limited Reg. No. 954009

A CIP catalogue record for this book is available from the British Library.

ISBN 0 7493 1501 6

Printed and bound in Great Britain by
Cox & Wyman Ltd, Reading, Berkshire

For Stephen, Georgia, Julia and Greg.

List of Illustrations

Contents

Acknowledgements

My first thanks must go to those patient and tolerant friends and members of my family on whom I inflicted my earliest thoughts and developing ideas and who gave me further insights. Many people acted as a sounding board but the book would not have been written without the particular encouragement and continuing support of my sisters and mother. I would also like to thank Alison Samuel who gave me advice on approaching publishers. I needed no other counsel.

Larraine Hills also needs a special mention. She offered the chance for me to refine and share the ideas more widely through the development of our Effective Parenting programme. More than that, she provided true friendship during the sometimes stressful production process.

Joan Freeman and David Hill willingly read the manuscript and made very helpful comments. Needless to say, responsibility for the content lies entirely with me.

Finally, I have to thank my immediate family who endured sharing their lives with the ever-present 'book'. I have learned much from them. I hope they forgive me my mistakes.

Preface

What I have to say in this book is a personal statement of my beliefs about what really matters in relationships with children. It represents the distillation of twenty-five years of trial and error, observation and contemplation – growing alongside first, my two stepchildren and then my own two children; of working with gifted children and their families; and of sharing experiences with a large number of other mothers, fathers and friends – sometimes singly and sometimes in groups. I believe that what I have discovered is common to all of us. I wish I had known what I now know twenty years ago. I am sharing it more widely in the hope that it will help others to negotiate more happily and confidently the minefield of parenthood. If we gain a sense of direction, and thereby raise our own personal self-esteem, we will be better able to reach our ultimate goal which has to be: raising children with self-esteem.

Introduction

Children – like adults – perform best when they feel good about themselves. And they feel good about themselves when someone tells them they have done well, are likeable and are good to be with. Only when a child is convinced that her parents love, like and cherish her, and are on her side, can she develop true self-esteem, and go on to become a self-confident, self-reliant and happy person.

This is a child-rearing book with a difference. It will not tell you how and when to potty-train, when to move your toddler into a bed, or when to introduce solid food. There are many excellent books offering advice about these matters. In fact, they are so comprehensive that some people looking at them, especially when they are pushed to their limits, feel inadequate and a failure. The very act of opening the book can ruin your confidence in sorting the problem out for yourself.

What is different about this book is that it concentrates on the relationship rather than the mechanics of child-rearing. It contains two simple core messages: first, trust yourself and your own instincts; and second, it is not so much *what* you do as *how you do it* that it important. Getting the approach right is much easier than most parents would believe. Once you realise that doing the best for your child comes down to creating in them self-esteem, self-confidence and self-reliance, then everything falls much more easily into place. What really matters is the relationship you build with your child. And it is surprisingly easy to help your child have these 'self' qualities. The key words, or things to remember, can be related to the word **'Expertise'**, using it as a memory jogger. This is explained in Chapter Five.

The book aims both to **encourage** and **empower**.

It will **encourage** because, no matter how many mistakes you have made in the past, or over how long a period, it offers a clear way forward. You can put the past behind you, forget guilt and apply this programme. It is, essentially, a valuable **tool kit**. But it can also act as a **repair kit** for anyone who is flat on the floor, whose children's behaviour is so awful it doesn't even get a mention in the 'bibles', for anyone who has lost all sense of direction and belief in their parental talents and even in themselves.

It will **empower**, because it hands the initiative back to you, the parent. It says that you can do it and that you don't need to lean on experts or books. The expertise lies within you. You should use the natural authority which you have as a parent. You should trust your own ability to decide what is the right thing to do, provided you have paid attention to the three targets – self-esteem, self-confidence and self-reliance. Immediately, your own self-esteem should improve and a virtuous circle can begin.

What is the book's message?

This book is all about self-esteem: what it is; why it is important to have it; what can go wrong if you don't have it; and, most important, how you can help your children to develop it. Unfortunately, in this society we seem to find it so much easier to do people down – to criticise, scold and reject – rather than to approve, praise and enjoy.

After twenty-five years of being both a mother and a stepmother and making mistakes; of reflecting on the behaviour of adults and trying to locate the source of their difficulties; and, more recently, of working with groups of parents to develop a better understanding of child-rearing issues and parenting styles, I have come to the conclusion that these three attributes are the starting points for happiness and security in later life.

'Self-esteem' is something of a growth industry at the moment. Rightly, more and more people are talking about and accepting the importance of having self-esteem for building successful work and other relationships and for having a fulfilled life. Lack of self-esteem is given increasingly as the reason why so many young people get themselves on the wrong side of the law, and why apparently successful media and business personalities are none the less unhappy and seem to be on an eternal search for the ultimate challenge, experience or security. There are now several management training courses based on improving self-esteem. Assertiveness courses, designed to develop personal confidence in both men and women, are also mushrooming. The therapy and counselling 'industries' would not be the size they are if everyone had a healthy and solid self-image. In all these contexts, self-esteem is treated as something which is only significant for adults. But if having good feelings about yourself, having enough self-confidence to meet and manage new experiences and take risks, and having the resources and resilience to cope with personal setbacks, are all so important, why not apply preventive strategies where the problem really starts – in childhood?

Having good self-esteem means that you have confidence in yourself: you know who you are, you like who you are, and you are content to face the world as you are. Self-esteem is the best gift any parent can give their child. Knowing yourself and liking yourself is so often the key to success in many modes of life – affecting personal relationships, general motivation and success in work. At the other end of the scale, low self-esteem can cause great anguish, heartache, under-achievement, bad behaviour, relationship problems and even depression.

Your own self-esteem is important, too. It is vital to look after yourself at the same time. Parents must continue to 'grow' alongside their offspring. You cannot put yourself into cold storage for the duration. You have to work at maintaining your own feelings of competence and self-esteem. If you are feeling low and inadequate, you are far less likely to help your child to flourish. Using the guidance on how to help your child feel good about herself, and inviting you to apply some of it to yourself as well as to your child, the book asks you to believe in yourself. Trust your instincts; trust your ability to do the job successfully; reclaim your authority; and rediscover and trust your common sense.

This is a practical handbook; but is not a detailed route map, giving you the answer to every little problem on the sometimes fraught and winding path of parenthood. It is, instead, more like a guide to map-reading, letting you choose the route. Feelings of self-esteem are influenced both by how the key people in your life relate to and treat you, and by your own achievements. By making parents more aware, through practical advice and examples, of what sort of behaviour makes anyone, regardless of age, feel good about themselves; and more aware of what behaviour acts as a 'put down' and damages feelings of self-worth, the book's purpose is then to pass the initiative back to you and say: do it your way. All you need to do is keep the three key targets in mind, and to check you are not breaking any of the ground rules.

The detail of child-rearing matters a great deal less than giving them this firm, secure foundation. Letting children know how far they can go, that there are limits to what you can give and what you will tolerate, and providing them with a structure and pattern of routines, will help to develop mutual trust and respect. This is the starting point for developing a strong and healthy identity. Encouraging feelings of self-worth in children starts with who they are – the personality that they were born with, encompassing their likes and dislikes. Everybody is different: you as a parent or carer have your own personality. You are who you are: so there can be no one way to bring up a child. This can be done, and should be done, in a million and one different ways. There are no magic answers. You have to discover what works for you, making mistakes along the way. That is inevitable and necessary. Provided that you pay attention to the fundamental rules which encourage self-esteem, self-confidence and self-reliance, and you are aware of the things which help or hinder children growing up feeling valued and wanted, a key message from this book is: it's OK to do it *your* way.

The main theme of this book is very simple, and is based on common sense rather than on any fancy 'ology'. Indeed, many parents will already be implementing some or all of the message, either intuitively or intentionally. What is new, I believe, is putting the ideas together to create a coherent framework which can act as a point of reference on most of the issues which arise in parenting, and can reveal some of the less obvious tactics we use to boost, or to put down, others.

Getting back in touch with our common sense will help us to:

- identify our own values;
- provide us and our children with a sense of direction;
- accept responsibility for guiding and leading our children into adulthood;
- avoid the extremes of child-rearing fashion and identify a more sustainable middle way.

We need, above all, to rediscover our natural parental authority.

How to use the book

Simple ideas are usually best presented in a simple way, and this is what I have attempted to do.

Chapter One looks at how, despite the special difficulties facing parents today, there is a way through which can rebuild our confidence and trust in ourselves.

Chapters Two and Three, 'The Tool Kit' and 'The Repair Kit', present an outline of the approach in a way which I hope is easy to understand. From then on, the book is 'layered'. In other words, the further you read into it, the deeper you can delve, moving beyond the core points and into some of the more complex dynamics of the parent-child relationship.

Chapter Four looks at where we, as parents, fit in. You could stop reading here and, I hope, still come out with some useful ideas.

Chapter Five introduces the Key Words which not only reinforce and distil the main message but also act as memory joggers. The words on their own say quite a lot, and each is followed by a short section which expands on the concept being presented, starting off with the main points and going on to consider them in more detail. Each 'key word' applies equally to the parent/carer and to the child. Each section is therefore split into two, looking first at how the word relates to the child's needs, and then how it relates to those of the parent(s). You can read as much or as little as you want to here, too.

Chapter Six, 'Words Matter', is for those who want to read and consider further still, and shows in more detail how and why we use words to put children down, and suggests other less hurtful ways of saying things.

Chapters Seven and Eight attempt to unravel the complexities of power, commitment and discipline in parenting, while still focusing on building self-esteem as the central aim.

Chapter Nine summarises what is meant by 'positive parenting' in the 'positive' and 'negative' behaviour circles which illustrate the cumulative effect of parental attitudes on the child.

Some repetition, therefore, is inevitable. Writing the book in this way I try to allow different people to take what they want from it; and also to reinforce, progressively, the ideas and their importance.

A simple truth can also be profound, as I hope I shall show.

One final word. Nobody should be put off by the number of suggestions for action. They are not all meant to be tried, and certainly not all of them at one go. The examples are given primarily for illustration and not for direction. As is suggested in Chapter Three, when you ask yourself at the end of the day what you have done to make your child feel good about herself, if you can give more positive than negative answers, that is good enough.

One
Trust Yourself: It's OK To Do It *Your* Way

Being a parent today is much harder than it was even ten years ago. There are several reasons why this is so.

Society is changing fast. Many people feel they have no coherent or relevant model for bringing up children in the 1990s. Today's parents will have come mostly from the smaller families more typical of recent times. While small families often provide greater material comforts and emotional benefits, the older children are usually so close in age to the younger ones that they either cannot, or are not needed to, help bring up or mind their much younger brothers or sisters. They therefore gain no early experience of child care which can be applied later with their own children – an experience which most world cultures offer. At the same time, and partly as a result of the same trend, the extended family is not there to play the same guiding or supporting role that it used to.

Many more people today are parenting alone, for a wide variety of reasons. The decisions and lifestyle changes which are entailed are so significant that they will inevitably cause some measure of stress and anxiety. Children make big demands, either directly, or indirectly through poor behaviour. Unsettling changes will increase those demands as they seek reassurance. If there is only one parent to meet these sometimes intense demands, the pressure will be that much more concentrated.

These social changes are happening in a context which puts even more pressure on parents. Today, we live in a climate of 'professionalism'. Having lost confidence in ourselves, not only do we look increasingly to 'professionals' to give us the answers to each and every one of our problems, but we also have ever higher standards and expectations of what we want to achieve in all the things we do. But we cannot meet these standards in everything we set out to do. When we inevitably fail, we are prone not just to guilt but also to further feelings of inadequacy and incompetence. Women especially can demand far too much of themselves.

In addition to this, many parents are trying to function in an authority void. In rejecting (rightly) the strict disciplinarian method of bringing up children, some parents have thrown away their authority and responsibility at the same time. Others have just lost their sense of direction and confidence in themselves. Someone who is confused and unsure will not command authority. Those who have consciously rejected the adult control which they themselves experienced in childhood in favour of a more child-centred approach now seem equally uncertain as to whether this alternative really works or gives children the best tools for coping and fitting in with the demands of education, work or families made on them later.

In the area of parenting, the relevant professionals are also telling us that what we do in these early years can have a big impact on the later personality of our child. This makes us increasingly anxious about making mistakes. Mothers are particularly prone to this type of anxiety. Believing it is our key job to provide our families with health and happiness, we not only worry about doing the job well, but also about the risk of causing psychological damage to our children.

And even that is not all. The state of marriages and partnerships is another pressure on us. We are all now constantly exposed to the expectation that we should have a high-quality sexual, emotional and social relationship with our partners and be 'happy'. The growing social acceptability of divorce and single parenthood seduces us into weighing up the state of our relationships more frequently, because if we judge that we do not have an ideal relationship, we have the option to abandon ship, get out and find something better elsewhere. With that possibility always hanging over both partners in the relationship, even if it is subconscious, men and women are having to bring up their children in a potentially explosive environment of insecurity and failure in which we demand too much and see too little. We are in danger of ignoring the obvious. Not only can we undervalue ourselves – our instincts and abilities – but worse, we can fail to realise, as we try to square the circle of modern life, that our children have basic needs too.

Just as adults perform best when they feel good about themselves and when others have shown they appreciate, love and care for them, so do children. A confident, trusting child, secure in her key relationships and conscious of her particular abilities and what it is that makes her unique, will play better, learn better, concentrate better and give, love and relate better. A child's sense of self develops from infancy. Therefore feelings about self-esteem, both good and bad, exist in childhood as strongly, or indeed more strongly, as they do in adulthood. Good self-esteem helps people to develop strong self-confidence. Self-confidence helps people become self-reliant and independent. These three attributes combine in individuals regardless of age to create human beings who are happy, productive, creative, flexible and, most important when considering the social context of our lives, giving.

These qualities lie at the heart of almost everything people say they want for themselves. Childhood is by far the best time to build self-esteem, self-confidence and self-reliance. If you do not obtain them then, it is much more difficult to acquire them as permanent features of yourself later. Where adults have relationship problems at home or at work, these are the things which they have often lacked. Where adults have other kinds of problems, and they are not handling them well, it is usually because their resilience and belief in themselves is low.

If you think of learning as human building blocks, these 'self' perceptions go down first and constitute a person's foundations. With strong foundations, we can weather the storms and earthquakes of life. Without them, we bend, creak, heave and crack. We can repair the cracks; but, if the foundations are weak, the cracks will only reappear. What this book sets out to do is show ways of laying these foundations.

As parents, if we want to find out how to be successful in our role, we need look no further than helping our children to develop confidence, self-reliance and, above all, good feelings about themselves. In terms of giving our children life-long advantages, anything else pales into insignificance. Other decisions in parenting, if they cannot be related to these objectives, are far less important. They are not worth getting fussed about. It matters far more that you:

- keep the parent-child relationship alive and on an even keel;
- maintain a consistent and predictable environment for your children;
- keep power play and damaging disputes to a minimum;
- demonstrate your commitment to them and show them that you understand them and are on their side.

There is no formula for being the perfect parent. There are no easy answers, and you will not find a convenient blueprint here. Success is much more about understanding and trusting yourself and your children, and bringing them up *your* way, consistently. You know your children better than anyone else can or does. You are able to do it, not because you are clever or good at it, not because you know the theory or the tricks, but because your children are yours. By showing that you understand them as only you can; by respecting their likes and dislikes and acknowledging their strengths and weaknesses which make them who they are; by treating them with the respect that we should all give to each other as human beings and demonstrating that you approve of them; you will help them to grow up with a strong sense of themselves, making them better able to withstand life's difficulties and to exploit life's challenges.

What we have to watch out for are the two demons: doubt and guilt. These are the two most destructive elements of any relationship. They are especially the enemies of a natural and fulfilled relationship with children, both because they reinforce uncertainty and insecurity and because they tempt you into an unhelpful regime of appeasement, or giving in. If we give in too often, we blur the boundaries. We teach our children that if they play on our guilt, they get their way. A small amount of guilt is healthy, but too much is definitely counter-productive. We all do make mistakes – through our over-concern, through stress or marital and relationship problems, through having to meet other family needs which often conflict. It is all right to make mistakes. If you can accept that you can mess things up, and the sky does not fall in when it happens, you will teach your children by example that it is also safe for them to make mistakes. If, on the other hand, you get crushed with a sense of failure, you teach them that making mistakes is something shameful and therefore to be avoided at all costs. Being able to take risks, and to accept both the possibility of and responsibility for making mistakes, is an absolute prerequisite for learning and healthy development.

Some of our mistakes are minor and do not matter. Others can cause temporary harm or hurt. But there are two vital things to remember that should relieve the agony of guilt. One is that, in the vast majority of parent-child relationships, you can make amends and undo the mistake even quite long after – so great is a child's need to be loved, trusted and respected by you – by apologising to them and repairing their self-image which will be damaged as a result. For years and years they can be the most forgiving creatures. They have to rely on you, so they want and need to believe in you.

The second vital thing is that if you are unpleasant to children, and have not seriously hurt them emotionally or physically, there is in place a cushion of love, a suspension of judgement, and so strong a wish, or need, to believe in you, that they and their relationship with you can take several knocks without significant damage. The danger only comes when that reserve of giving you the benefit of the doubt is used up. Then, to protect themselves from the uncomfortable conclusion that they are not worth loving, they separate themselves from you emotionally and are no longer willing to play any part in a relationship which exposes them to such anguish. This is what Bruno Bettelheim, the eminent child psychologist, and D.W. Winnicott, a paediatrician and psychoanalyst, meant when they talked about being 'a good enough' mother or parent. Provided you are not near the danger point, and you have loved your children in a way which has convinced them of it, there is room for error, and repair, repeatedly.

So, trust yourself. You and your children have a unique relationship. And they adore you, love you and need you more than you can know. No-one else can take your place as their mother or father. This is the fundamentally encouraging reality. Each relationship has to be not only different but also unique. You are you, with all of your strengths and weaknesses which you carry with you; and the child has her own unique personality from day one, which can be influenced, but you try to change it at your peril! You have to work with what you have collectively got. Quite apart from that, there are partners and siblings who will alter the chemistry of what's possible to do within your family. No-one can tell you precisely what will work for you two or even, at a more complex level, what will work within the whole family – taking other family members' values and boundaries or tolerances into account. Only you can know all this and put it all into the equation of compromise. The answer does not lie out there in an encyclopaedia. It lies, and has to lie, within ourselves. You have to work out what works for you. And what works for you is OK. If it is working, don't listen to anyone else telling you that you should be doing it differently. If it is working, without you needing to behave like a dictator, and your child does not have significant problems of bad or anxiety-driven behaviour, it is probably working because you are getting the essentials right – giving your child love, respect and security. The finer details do not matter.

But the essentials do matter. This book presents these as a tool kit, and summarises the necessary techniques through the scheme of 'The Expertise' in Chapter Five. It shows you how to *get* 'The Expertise', and *forget* the guilt!

Two
Building a Firm Foundation: I The Tool Kit

Self-esteem, self-confidence and self-reliance

All parents *want the best* for their child, and they also start out wanting *to do the best* for their child. That is why many people, on becoming parents for the first time, head for the bookshops, libraries or magazine racks to find out how to do it. Unfortunately, babies do not come with instructions.

Wanting the best

Most parents would agree that the most important thing they want for their child is happiness. But what brings happiness? Different people will have very different ideas about this. Many will see happiness as something you feel as a *result* of some other desirable situation. Therefore, when parents are asked the question: 'What do you want for your children as they grow up?', they are more likely to answer 'To do well', 'Not to want for anything', 'To have plenty of toys to play with', or 'To keep themselves busy'. When asked about the longer term, when their children have become independent adults, the answers will be along the lines of 'Success', 'To be well thought of', 'To have plenty of money', 'To get married and have children', 'To have an interesting life' and so on. We tend to think partly in terms of things which would bring us as individuals a sense of achievement, assuming that achievement in itself brings happiness; and partly in terms of activities which would make us, as parents, feel proud of our children. Parents also, commonly, have ambitions for their children which avoid the mistakes they feel they have made in their own lives. They want their children to 'better themselves' or 'not to do as I did'. By encouraging their children to achieve, in whatever terms they define, they think they are fulfilling their duty to deliver happiness. But are they? Is happiness something which parents have within their power to give to their children?

True happiness, it has been said, is not a place of arrival, it is a manner of travelling. If happiness is seen as something which you have to go out and find or buy, and can arrive at, by the same token it can also disappear. That kind of acquired happiness certainly exists but it is, by definition, external, transient and fragile. There is a deeper-rooted, more permanent happiness to be experienced which is internal. Whether or not you have it depends upon how comfortable you are with yourself. This is self-esteem. 'Happiness is Self Contentedness' wrote the Greek philosopher Aristotle some three hundred years before the birth of Christ.

Parents can and do have a major influence over whether their children possess or experience self-contentedness. Doing the best for your children means helping them to experience good feelings about themselves: feelings of self-worth, and feelings of competence gained through the development of self-confidence and self-reliance.

Self-esteem

What is 'self-esteem'?

Self-esteem relates to:

- self-image
- self-contentedness
- self-acceptance
- self-worth
- self-approval

Self-esteem means feeling good about yourself. It means liking yourself and being content with, and even proud of, who you are. If you have self-esteem, you are happy to be you and you believe in your intrinsic value as a unique individual. It therefore involves having a positive self-image and an accurate self-awareness. You know who you are, and you can accept who you are without fear, embarrassment or doubt because you accept all of it. You like enough of yourself to be able to live with the bits which you find less endearing. If you know you are good at some things, it helps you acknowledge, without any loss to your self-image, that you are not so good at other things. Taken together, they help you to open up your whole self to the world outside. Nothing needs to be hidden or suppressed. Self-esteem is also self-sustaining. It is like having an electrical generator inside. When you feel low, or run down, you can recharge your own batteries. People without good self-esteem find it much harder to do this themselves. They need another power source to recharge them. They may find this in other people, or in situations which challenge them and give them feelings of worth and achievement. People with poor self-esteem are constantly on the lookout for where they can get their next power fix from. If they are feeling *really* low, they will not even allow others near enough to 'refuel' them, and they sometimes end up throwing themselves away as a spent force.

Good self-esteem, therefore, is:

- liberating
- calming
- regenerating
- self-sustaining

Why is it important to develop good self-esteem?

Self-esteem helps to give us:

- happiness
- resilience
- creativity
- the ability to take risks
- flexibility and adaptability
- the ability to give and commit to others
- common sense

If you are **resilient**, you do not go to pieces when faced with difficult and unexpected challenges. You can offer help and stability to others when they need support. Life is full of disappointments and difficulties. If we can give our children the tools to survive knocks and to bounce back, we will have given them something of life-long value.

If you are **creative**, you have the ability to think of different ways to manage situations. You are a problem-solver not a problem-builder. Being able to see your way round and through problems is a great advantage. Problem-builders do not get very far, and they may find that their friends and acquaintances soon tire of their negative attitudes.

If you are **able to take risks**, you can try new things without being frightened of failing or of not being able to manage unforseen events. This means you can go on learning, discovering and developing yourself to your life's end.

If you can be **flexible and adaptable**, you will be able to sustain longer and more rewarding relationships, enjoy the unknown, use what you know in different circumstances, and be better prepared for life in this increasingly fast-changing world.

If you are able **to give and to commit**, your experiences and relationships will be enriched. The more you put into something, the more you will get out of it. People who cannot commit and who keep themselves on the outside may feel 'safe' from disappointments or having to expose themselves, but they will remain isolated and will have a poorer life for it.

If you have sound **common sense**, you have an inner 'library' of views and practical experiences which offer you generalised guidance in any situation you may come across. It provides a sense of direction and a feeling of security, knowing that your overall 'view of the world' will guide you when there is no-one else to consult.

How do you get good self-esteem?

Self-esteem comes from others:

- valuing you
- approving of you
- spending time with you
- understanding you
- trusting you
- respecting you
- being committed to you
- being 'on your side'

The only way infants or young children can discover themselves and believe that they are likeable and lovable is through having someone else responding to them; liking and loving them and understanding their needs and feelings. That someone else has to be the key and regular carer, who is invariably the mother. This is the bottom line. They believe in themselves if, and only if, others have given them reason to believe that they are worth caring for, are good to be with and are worth sticking up for: if someone else has been committed to them and been seen to be on their side. Robust, permanent, or 'core' self-esteem can only be developed if those on whom they rely and whom they trust and adore *demonstrate clearly* to them *and in their own terms* that they are esteemed.

Very young children have to interpret their world through their parents and significant carers. How they are treated and how they *feel* they are treated, are potent ingredients in the process of developing their identity. Through offering structure, parents create order out of what can be a terrifying chaos. Through order, infants can learn to predict. Through having their needs acknowledged and met, infants learn that they and their judgements can be trusted, and they learn to trust in return. It is not enough for a parent to say, 'But I love them. Surely they realise that?' We have to break down into separate activities all the ways in which children interpret love.

Children receive messages from us all the time. Inevitably these are both good and bad. We cannot say the right things all the time. We will be more or less tolerant, kind or thoughtful depending upon our state of mind. This begins to matter only when the negative and 'put down' messages significantly outweigh the supportive and understanding ones. Later, when the child begins to socialise and spend time with a wider circle of people, the messages can be received from a variety of sources. They will still rely on you for their core self-image, but it will be reinforced, refined or even revised through their relationships with others.

Can a poor self-image gained in the early years be overturned later? If you have spent most of your early years getting bad messages about yourself, and then others outside the family begin to tell you something different because they have found things they like about you, what will be the effect? At first, you won't believe it. This negative reaction is likely to go on for some time. How can you overturn your perception of yourself with just a few instances of 'flattery', for that is how it will be perceived. When it has been said often enough (and it *will* have to be said often) you will begin to rate yourself more highly. For the first time, you will have experienced the intoxicating pleasure of feeling good about yourself. But research shows that this kind of praise has to be given often for the recipient to remain convinced.

Getting started

How can you help your children to develop a clear and positive self-image? A good starting point is to identify what makes each of your children unique – what makes them who they are:

Step One Write down what you think their personality is – strengths and weaknesses. Include those bits you would prefer not to be there. If you are feeling particularly negative about them, get someone else who knows them well to sit down with you and make you realise they have good features too.

For example, *your child:*

adapts easily to new situations
cares deeply about things
is quick to cry
finds it hard to concentrate
finds it hard to share things
likes to be involved in 'real' jobs
lives in a fantasy world
is very resilient
is generous
likes quiet time
does not like to be interrupted
likes playing with younger children
finds it hard to tell the truth
is tidy/untidy

Step Two See if you can find any connection between the things which you like and those which you do not care for so much. They may be two sides of the same coin.

***For example**, you may like the way they are quick to make choices, take decisions and seem to know their mind, but not like the way they constantly argue about doing things their way. But isn't this part of the same thing? You may like the way they can stand up for themselves when playing with their friends, but not like it when they are assertive with you. Again, isn't this the same strength coming out in a different place?*
Think positive!

Step Three Write down their likes and dislikes; things that they like to do, things they like to or won't eat, their favourite clothes, and how they like to spend their time. This will add another dimension to your understanding of who they are.
If you can identify lots of things they don't like, and very few things they do like, it is time to take improving their self-esteem very seriously. Children who do not have a clear idea of themselves will find it much easier to 'define themselves by the negative'. In other words, to establish their difference, they will say they are *not* like someone else, particularly their siblings. By a process of deduction, they will end up with some kind of picture of themselves. But it is far healthier if someone can say straight away: 'I am *this* sort of a person', rather than slice away at what they are *not* and see what is left.

Step Four Think how you can give them space to be themselves, to do the things which they like to do.

***For example**, if they enjoy having time on their own, have you kept their brothers and sisters out of their* *hair? Have you taught the others to respect that wish to be undisturbed? If they like playing their favourite game with you, have you made yourself available to do it? If they like football or swimming, do you make sure they get the chance to do them?*

Step Five Tell them from time to time what it is you like about them, and do not just say that it is because they have been 'good'. Spell it out for them so that they realise you understand them and they get a clearer picture of who they are. Help them to feel proud of themselves.

Some further suggestions once you are underway:

Value them. How?

- Let them know that you realise they are good at certain things, and ask for their help using these skills wherever appropriate. *'You are good with your hands. Could you help me mend this . . . ?'*
- Show them that you enjoy being with them. *'I enjoyed our trip to the shops together.'*
- Listen to them properly when they want to tell you something.

Approve of and praise them. How?

- Say that you like their ideas. *'That was a good idea of something to do.' 'I wouldn't have thought of doing it that way. That was inventive.'*
- Show that you like their choice of friends. *'Tracey's a good friend. We must have her round again soon.'*
- Show that you like how they choose to dress. *'That jumper looks good with those trousers. You chose well this morning.'*
- Tell them when you think they have done something well. It means more to a child if you praise

them for something specific which they have done well, rather than blanket praise.

For example, *'It was a lovely surprise for me that you laid the table/cleared away the toys.' 'Thanks for letting me know in good time about going out before supper tonight', both say much more than 'You are a good girl/boy'.*

- Reward them with praise and your attention rather than with presents, unless the presents come as an unusual surprise. Material rewards can too easily become something the child negotiates and manipulates.

Spend time with them. How?

- Alone with them.
- On their terms, doing what they want to do. *'It's half an hour until tea. What would you like us to play?*
- On your terms. *'Come and talk to me while I/help me to sort out this cupboard.'*

Show you understand them. How?

- Try to imagine how they will be feeling about something and voice it: tell them how you think it might be for them. *'It must have been really embarrassing for you to have left your dinner money at home again.' 'I know you don't enjoy tidying your room but you can't see where to tread safely.'*
- Do not treat every child in the family the same. Although it is important to be seen to be fair in your overall handling, identical treatment ignores their separate identities and personalities.

Trust them. How?

- Give them appropriate (in terms of their age) responsibilities, and assume that they will carry them out. For example, brushing their teeth, putting used clothes in the wash-basket, getting themselves dressed in the morning. This will also develop a wider sense of responsibility and will encourage independence.

- If they feel strongly about something, trust them to know themselves and let them influence what happens to them. This will apply to such things as friendships, how much they want to eat, how warm or cold they are feeling.
- Assume they know the rules and your expectations. If you say 'Don't forget to . . .', or 'You will remember to . . .' you are actually stating that they cannot be treated as responsible. You are as likely to challenge them to defiance as to get the desired result.
- Assume that they will be able to be independent from you, but be accessible if they need you.
- Don't hover over them when they are trying to do something new, or help them with it – unless they ask you to.

Respect them. How?

- Be willing to compromise. Children sometimes have valid reasons for disagreeing. You do not undermine your authority by sometimes letting them 'win'. In fact, you increase your authority. (See 'Compromise', Chapter Five).
- Listen to them.
- Give them choices to allow some self-determination and autonomy.
- Be seen to be fair.
- Apologise to them if you know you have been unreasonable.

Show your commitment to them. How?

- Spend time with them.
- Play with them.
- Talk to them.

- Support them, at school and in things they like to do.
- Be there for them.

Be on their side. How?

- Be their last point of refuge in distress, their safety net, somewhere to hide and, when they need it, their friend.
- By doing at least one thing from each of the above categories.

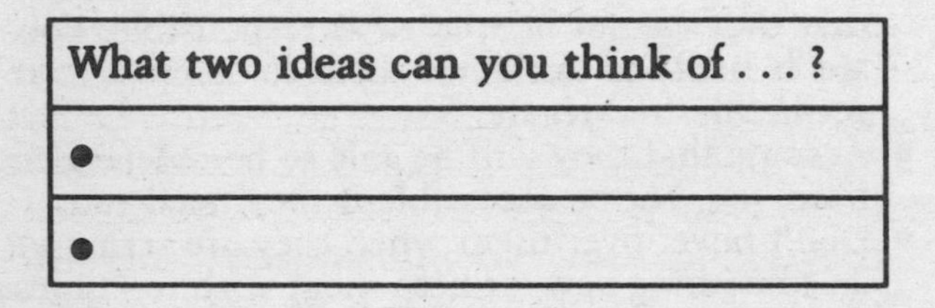

What two ideas can you think of . . . ?
•
•

(For more on Praise, Trust, Time, etc., see Chapter Five.)

What else can you do? The idea of 'the balanced activity diet'

These days, parents are only too familiar with health experts telling them to feed their children properly. We are told that by the age of eight children are already affecting their adult life expectancy by what they eat and how much exercise they take. We are being persuaded to reduce the dependence on sugar and fat and instead give them a more balanced diet to include vegetables, fruit, carbohydrate and proteins.

In the same way, we should look at how our children spend their time. The greater the variety of things they do and enjoy doing, the better will they know themselves, discover talents and be able to use their time as adults, and the more well-rounded and fulfilled they will be.

The balanced activity diet can have a profound and important impact on self-esteem as well. The more spheres the child can try, the more she is likely not only to find something which she can be good at to make her feel proud, but also to have the chance to be herself, to try out herself, in many different ways. For example, a child who watches television all the time is likely to have very little idea about the full range of her capabilities. A child gifted at playing the piano, and who does little else, will have little idea about her other talents or interests. If at any stage she decides to stop playing, she could be left with a very uncomfortable void. The child who is fanatical about sports but later receives a permanent injury preventing him from doing anything, will similarly be left with a void. It is just as true, then, with pastimes which are generally approved of as with those, like watching television or playing video games, which are sometimes frowned upon: a single interest which crowds out others encourages the child to begin to rely on that for their sense of security because it is familiar and safe territory. It does nothing to encourage the degree of social flexibility and confidence which takes much of the anxiety out of new situations – a real advantage in today's changing world. A single interest – or, even worse, inactivity – does not help your child to develop the confidence to take risks, other than, perhaps, the death-defying risks of bravado which children needing instant acclaim and attention from their peers are willing to flaunt.

Bruno Bettelheim warned parents against implementing a contrived 'balanced diet' of activities because it is too controlling and may deny their children time for free play. Free play certainly is absolutely vital for the development of children's self-esteem. But the idea of the balanced diet is still useful and valid if parents make sure that there is some time when children *are* left alone to develop their imaginations, to play freely through their anxieties in the way in which they feel they need to at the time. Denying a child the chance to play has similar effects to not allowing an adult the chance to sleep and dream. Their sense of reality can become distorted. Like night-dreams, day-dreams and fantasy play are fundamental ways of re-establishing emotional equilibrium. (See Play, page 107.)

What does a balanced diet look like?

- **outdoor** things (walks, tree-climbing, visits to the park, i.e., physical things; playing anything outside)
- **creative** things (drawing, painting, modelling, e.g., with Playdoh, sand, water, cooking, gardening, making and hearing music)
- **social** things (visits to friends and relatives – your friends too so they can learn how to socialise from you)
- **imaginative** things (playing indoor 'tents' with blankets, or trains with cardboard boxes, 'let's pretend' games such as doctors or schools)
- **ball** skills and games
- **unstructured** play (let them fiddle around in a seemingly disorganised way with anything or nothing so that their thoughts can wander at will)
- **bookish** things (read to them, look at pictures in books or magazines, library trips. Let them be with you if you are reading or writing so that they have the model to copy)
- **number** things (counting as part of daily life – stairs, spoons to lay on the table, steps to reach the next lamppost, houses to the postbox, etc.)

What are the essential things to avoid if you want your child to have 'good' self-esteem?

Even if you are doing many of the things suggested above, it is still important to be aware of the responses and behaviours we commonly use which damage a child's self-esteem. Knowing what undermines children means, first, that they can be avoided and, second, that if we do say or do something hurtful (which we all do from time to time), we recognise it and can make up for it by going out of our way to repair the damage. Children are very sensitive to criticism. They seem to take it much more to heart than praise. It may therefore take two or three 'boosters', or 'puff-ups' to undo the damage of one insult or 'put-down' and to restore 'ego equilibrium'.

So what should be avoided?

Making approval or love conditional on good behaviour

Children need to be loved for who they are, warts and all, not only when they are well-behaved – when they are being who *you want them to be.*

Combining and confusing disapproval of things done with disapproval of the person

When they stray outside the boundaries you have set for them, always make it clear that you are complaining about *what they have done,* not *who they are.* 'That was a silly thing to do', not 'You are so silly'.

Blaming them for things which go wrong: 'It's your fault.'

Children are easy targets for blame. It is strangely comforting for us to be able to shirk our responsibility for things which go wrong and instead point our finger at the child who happened to be around. While children should, in some situations, be held responsible for their behaviour, much of the time either they are too young to realise what was going to be the result of their mistakes, or they had very little, directly, to do with the complained of calamity. *'It's your fault. If you hadn't got me angry, I wouldn't have dropped the plate!'* Blame directs responsibility away from the blamer and on to the blamed. Blame creates guilt and shame which, for children, are complex, confusing and restricting emotions.

Putting them down

'Put-downs' take many forms. These are explored and analysed in detail in Chapter Six. They include criticisms, physical rejections, threats, blame, labels such as 'You are useless', lack of trust, and so on. Adults are often completely unaware of the impact of their clumsy words. Children are so keen to have the approval of those they care about that even minor criticisms can be quite hurtful.

Self-esteem: question check-list

The questions listed below are to be used as a guide *either* if you are not sure what to do in a given situation, *or* just to reflect on the day to see if you are still moving in the right direction. If you are not sure what to do at any time, you do not necessarily need to go to books on the subject, or to spend time on the telephone finding out what your friends would do if they were you. The questions can be seen as a kind of yardstick against which you can check your own common sense ideas and work things out for yourself. If your idea does not get a 'yes' answer to any of the questions below, then you should think again. If it does, then it is OK to do it your way.

- **Will this make them feel good, or at least not bad, about themselves?**
- **Have I shown that I have understood their feelings and/or point of view on anything today?**
- **Have I shown any interest in, or asked about, anything they have done today?**
- **Have I listened to them with my whole hearted attention, at least once?**
- **Will they think that I am on their side?**

Conclusion

Children can value, esteem and love themselves only if you have convinced them that you have valued, esteemed and loved them first.

Self-confidence

What is self-confidence?

Self-confidence is:

- trusting your ability to form and sustain relationships
- trusting your ability to complete various tasks well
- knowing that others value your abilities
- trusting your ability to manage new situations
- trusting your own judgements and common sense

Self-confidence is close to but clearly different from self-esteem. Self-esteem, it has been stated, relates to a belief in one's intrinsic worth. It involves a view of your inner self as seen by you from the outside. Self-confidence, by contrast, relates to a judgement about your abilities in the wider world. It involves a view of yourself operating in society, as seen by you from the inside. In answer to the question, 'Who trusts me and believes in me?' the answer is a triumphant, 'I trust and believe in myself!' Following on from this is an expectation that others will have the same confidence in you.

Trust is a key element of self-confidence. The *Oxford English Dictionary* defines 'confidence' as: 'firm trust; assured expectation; boldness'. Nobody can develop self-confidence if they neither trust themselves nor have an 'assured expectation' about the (therefore predictable and trustworthy) behaviour of others. Children who do not have a measure of consistency and predictability in their lives will find it very hard to acquire the necessary trust either in others or in themselves to become self-confident.

On the other hand, if those who are most important to you clearly trust you and provide a consistent environment, you can begin to trust yourself, your judgements and the behaviour and decisions of others around you. This is the beginning of common sense – applying your knowledge of the predictable world around you, knowing something about yourself and how to relate to others. Self-confidence means that you are confident not merely that your parents like, love and want you but that others show interest in, appreciate and want to spend time with you, too. It is your wider acceptability, by your peers and others, that is crucial, too. It is something which therefore develops after infancy, when children begin to socialise outside the familiar environment of their family.

Natural self-confidence comes from within. But self-confidence is also something which people can create, and often do create, on top of doubts about their core self. We can acquire skills and accomplishments. We can learn to entertain and amuse. We can discover techniques to control and to avoid many of life's uncertainties. We can, through later experience and observation, develop and supplement social skills. We all build on and enrich ourselves as we live our lives, gaining knowledge and insights as well as confidence as we mature. This is the joy of living. Teaching our children how to unfold or unwrap themselves to discover new treasures and talents within them, much as they do in the game 'pass the parcel'; to learn to trust themselves and their abilities in new situations, is something of great value which will give them life-long benefit.

Why is it important to develop self-confidence?

Self-confidence helps us to be:

- open and outgoing
- straightforward
- trusting
- trustworthy and reliable
- determined and able to stick at things

How do children acquire self-confidence?

Self-confidence comes from:

- being accepted for who you are
- having someone show confidence in you
- knowing there is something you are good at
- having firm expectations of other people's behaviour
- not having too many experiences of failure
- not being afraid of failing
- developing competence with the safety of a parent close by
- seeing others you admire and copy being confident and happy

Getting started

There are three necessary components of self-confidence. If you think that you need to boost your child's self-confidence, you will need to take action to encourage each one. The three components are: Trust and Predictability; Competence; Sociability.

Trust and Predictability

Step One Routines are important for developing feelings of trust and security. Think about the routines and relationships between you and your family and your friends. How much do they keep to a pattern? Will your child begin each day with a reasonably clear idea of what will happen and when, either in terms of events, or who they will meet? How predictable are the relationships in their lives? Do they see certain people regularly, or do they come and go in an apparently unplanned and arbitrary way? Are the relationships which they have with the adults and children around them ones which they can trust, or do the people involved – including, perhaps, you – 'blow hot and cold on them' in a way which they will see as unexpected? How predictable is *their* behaviour?

Step Two If you can see that there are things in your lives which your child will not easily be able to predict:

- think if there is anything you could change about your own or their commitments to increase the sense of pattern and 'assured expectation' in their life;
- if there is not much that is within your control to change, make sure that you explain in advance both *why* things have to happen in the way that they do, and *what* is going to happen on any particular day;
- speak to the relevant people about making either the *frequency* or the *content* of their visits more predictable. This will be especially important if children are visited by a parent who no longer lives with them.

Competence (being good at things)

Step One Under the headings of different skills, list the things which you think your child is good at and which he likes to do and make him feel good. These skills can be:

practical e.g., seeing how to make or mend things, and build things;

physical e.g., good at sport (kicking/catching balls, swimming, running, etc.);

mental e.g., having good ideas about things, being good at solving practical problems, good at school work;

social e.g., good at playing with others; kind and considerate; good at making new friends; sensing when people need to be left alone or quiet;

process e.g., being good at trying new things, sticking at difficult tasks etc.

Step Two Ask *them* what they like doing and what they think they are good at. It will be very interesting to learn if these are the same things which you have written down. It is quite likely they will be the same, because children will naturally value themselves for the same things which they have realised you value in them. If there are things which you have listed and they have not, make sure you let them know your feelings about what they are good at. If they have listed things which you have not, ask yourself why. Is it because you have a different set of values? Can you adjust these to accept their view of themselves? If you see these attributes as negative (for example, they might say they are good at fighting), consider whether they are already judging themselves outside your scales because they feel they cannot measure up to your expectations. For interest's sake, try the same exercise with the things they are not so good at.

Step Three If neither you nor they have been able to identify a range of things they are competent at, offer them chances to try new skills. Everyone needs to feel good at something. Find out from the library or local sports centre what children's activities are available in your area.

Sociability

Step One Trust and develop their social skills. Involve them moderately in your social life. If you have them with you, it shows not only that you are happy to be with them but also that you trust that they will behave sensibly and appropriately. Getting used to being in new situations, and learning to talk with different people, will increase their confidence considerably. Keep it in proportion, though. If you do it too much, they might not appreciate your boundaries and learn that you are entitled to your own time, without them. Give them advance warning of your feelings – of bad temper, tiredness, sadness, frustration or whatever. *'I've had a difficult day at work today. I might be snappy. It might be best for you if you steer clear of me for a while.'* Or *'I've had an argument with X today and I'm feeling rather sore. If I rat at you, don't take it seriously.'* This not only teaches them techniques for managing their own feelings, but also gives them a chance to learn sensitivity to the feelings and moods of others, and to accommodate and adjust as appropriate. These are essential social skills, immensely valuable for later life, and even for their lives at home or at school here and now.

Step Two Encourage them to play, with you and others in the family, and with friends. Restrict the use of pastimes, for example television and video games, which do not necessarily involve talking, sharing and compromise, i.e., social interaction.

Some further suggestions once you are underway

Trust and Predictability

Chart all changes. Give as much advance warning of changes as possible.

If possible, **introduce big changes little by little**, so change is not an uncomfortable and frightening experience. Introduce changes one at a time. For example, don't ask your child to cope with starting school and you going back to work, or changing your work routines, at the same time.

Make sure that the 'do's and don'ts' **rules for your family are enforced consistently**. If they are not, maybe you have too many. Write down which ones are most important to you, ensure everyone is clear what you expect of them, and then make sure that they comply! If you don't think you have any rules, and life can get chaotic at times, then make some. All children need boundaries; that is, limits beyond which they know they should not go.

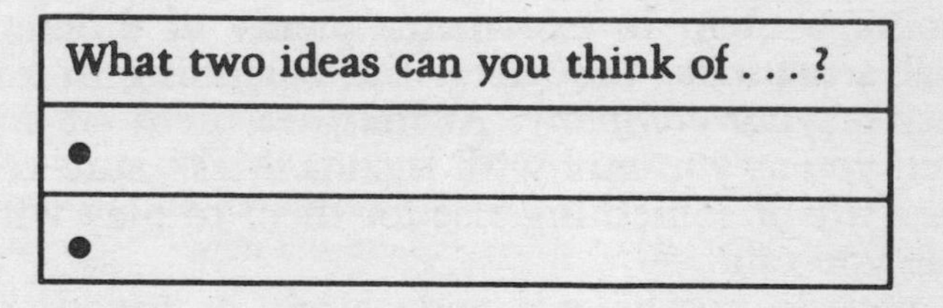

What two ideas can you think of . . . ?
•
•

Competence

Ask for their help with something they are good at to show that you appreciate their skill. For example, if they are good at thinking things out, you can ask them to help you with a decision you have to make. If they are practical, invite them to help you mend something. If they are strong and well co-ordinated, ask them to help you lift or move things.

Acknowledge their pride in their achievements. Wherever you can, reinforce their own good feelings about themselves. *'You must have felt really proud when you managed to do that.' 'I bet that made you feel good!'*

When they are trying something new, **let them know that you believe that they can do it**. Let them see that you have confidence in them.

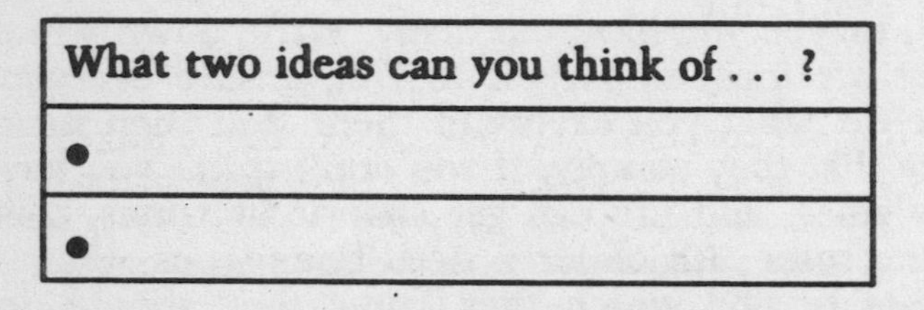
What two ideas can you think of . . . ?

-
-

Sociability

Encourage them to **experience plenty of different social situations**, though at the beginning in *the safety of your company*. At first, let them sit and watch you as you mix with friends. Make sure you take a toy or something else for them to play with while you talk.

If you do not have a wide circle of friends or a range of things which you do, **see if you can take them places where there are other children**, for example a playgroup or the playground. Perhaps you could suggest getting together with a neighbour for a cup of tea, or go and visit someone in your family. Local libraries often run story times in the afternoon for under-fives. They will also have information about other activities in the area for small children and for parents feeling alone.

What two ideas can you think of? . . .
•
•

What are the important things to avoid?

- Do not undermine their feelings about their own ability.
- Do not burst their bubble of confidence if they believe they can do something.
- Do not constantly tell them that other children, or you, can do whatever they have done better.
- Do not confuse being confident in their ability to manage without you with abdicating responsibility.
- Do not question their ability to be a good friend to others or, indeed, to themselves.

Self-confidence: question check-list

Just as with self-esteem, the questions listed below are to be used as a guide *either* if you are not sure what to do in a given situation, *or* just to reflect on the day to see if you are offering enough scope for the development of confidence.

- Have I given them the chance to do something they are good at?
- Have I valued anything that they think they have done well?
- Have I acknowledged their own feelings of achievement (even if *I* think they could have done better)?

- Have I given them a chance to socialise in a variety of different situations, with both their own friends and with mine?
- Have I demonstrated my confidence in their ability to cope with and function in the world out there by taking them with me when I go out?
- When they had to do something new for the first time, did I offer them the security of being close by? Did I acknowledge their worries about it, and did I show confidence in their ability to cope? Did I praise them afterwards for having managed the situation well?
- How predictable and structured is their life at the moment? Have I kept them properly informed of and explained any changes and upsets?
- Can I introduce any routines which will create a greater sense of pattern, consistency and security to their lives?

Conclusion

Children will develop self-confidence only if you have first shown trust and confidence in them and have provided an environment within which they can predict and trust.

Self-reliance

What is self-reliance?

Self-reliance is the ability to manage on your own: to know how to manage your time, to function and think independently, combined with the ability to take risks and to solve problems. With self-reliance, there is no need for other people's approval before moving forward or doing something new. There is no need, either, for detailed and constant guidance on how to achieve the end product. You can rely on yourself. Self-reliance is about tasks and skills – knowing how to do things, how to achieve things, or how to manage things. But is also covers the ability both to be alone and to think things through on your own.

Self-reliance is broader than self-confidence. Self-confidence relates to what we can do, to specific skills and aptitudes. Self-reliance is about being **independent, creative** and **self-sufficient**; having confidence, if you like, in our inner resources to enable us as individuals to adapt and manage on our own.

Why is it important to develop self-reliance?

Self-reliance helps us to be:

- active
- independent
- creative
- competent
- spontaneous

Self-reliance is also about having confidence in your own ideas. It is about being able to carry things through to completion. It is about having a certain degree of physical competence so that lack of strength or co-ordination will never stand in the way of achieving your target. It is about not being frightened of setting yourself goals, and not being hamstrung by fear of failure.

There is a common aphorism in management training that the world is divided into three types of people:

- those who make things happen;
- those who watch things happening;
- those who notice nothing until after and then ask 'what's happened?'.

Those who have good self-reliance (and confidence

and self-esteem) are the people who make things happen.

If we want our children to be able to make things happen, we do not have to think of this on a big, earth-shattering scale. It does not mean that we all should want our children to be captains of industry, Nobel scientists or literary geniuses. We should not seek to have them achieve on a scale which makes a difference to *others*. What it does mean is that we should aim to give our children a degree of self-reliance which enables them to keep a better control of *their* lives and keep open choices for *them*. This should enhance the quality of their life. Also, we live in a society which is changing so fast that the successful individuals of the future will be the ones who can both cope with change and contribute to it; in other words, those who can show flexibility, initiative and creativity.

Self-reliant at what?

We can encourage self-reliance from quite an early age, within our own homes. As soon as children show that they can manage things for themselves, however slowly, clumsily or imperfectly, we should give them opportunities to do so. Self-reliance is best introduced and experienced stage by stage, starting early and building it up gradually as children become more competent and responsible. When children are very young, they have a virtually unstoppable drive to become independent. Before they are confronted with adult concepts of failure, they are willing to try and try again until they master the task in view. They desperately want to lose their dependency and become free, like adults or older siblings, to do things on their own. The passion with which a parent's help is sometimes rejected has to be seen to be believed! If we stand in the way of letting them try, or transmit frustration or disapproval when they do not quite do it right, we will sap their growing sense of potency and damage their belief in themselves. The more we do for them, the more we actively prevent them from developing the habit of making judgements and decisions for themselves. We turn them into automatons who can only act when instructed. The stages of developing self-reliance will look something like this:

First Stage Managing their own life and person: e.g., feeding, toileting, washing, cleaning teeth, getting dressed. As soon as babies are able to get some food into their mouths by their own hands, they should be encouraged to do it. As soon as they are able to tell, most of the time, when they need a wee, we should give them the responsibility to manage this. If we keep overall control at this stage, we will be saying that they cannot be trusted. By the time children start school, they should be wiping their own bottoms and dressing themselves.

Second Stage Carrying out their own ideas and directing their own play.

Third Stage Managing things within the home and taking responsibility for:

- some domestic chores: for example, keeping their rooms tidy, putting their used clothes in the wash-basket, laying the table;
- organising how they occupy and entertain themselves within agreed guidelines;
- managing their own pocket money.

By this time, children should be allowed to be involved in the decisions which affect their lives, for example, spending pocket money how they wish, which after-school activities they take up, agreeing contracts specifying rewards granted for extra responsibilities and commitments.

Fourth Stage Managing themselves outside the home: e.g., school, homework, getting their things ready, their social life, out-of-school clubs and activities, music lessons, etc.

Fifth Stage Managing others within and outside the home: e.g., babysitting.

Letting Go

Clearly, you cannot encourage self-reliance in your children if you are not prepared to stand back and, progressively, **let go**. Doing that in the right amounts, and at the right time, is very hard to judge. How much responsibility and independence you give should, of necessity, depend on the age and personality of each child and on your own circumstances. Giving them too much of either before they are *emotionally or developmentally* ready for it can be as damaging as not giving them enough.

Letting go too late Some parents believe they have to prove their devotion and commitment by waiting on their offspring hand and foot. Indeed, this is a crucial part of their definition of being a good parent. But they are fundamentally mistaken. What they are really proving is their need to feel needed, not their devotion. They are hooking their child like a fisherman, keeping a line out on them and winding them in from time to time, jerking them to the bank, just to prove that they are still in control.

Letting go too soon If children get too much independence too soon when they still need support and attention, they will feel abandoned and shamed, not independent and proud.

How do children become self-reliant?

Self-reliance comes through having:

- responsibility
- independence
- relevant experience
- scope for self-determination
- autonomy
- common sense
- problem-solving skills
- practical skills
- good health

Responsibility

Responsibility means having the job of carrying something out, and being held accountable for it. This differs from independence, which involves taking decisions about how, where and when that task should be carried out. Children should grow up with appropriate and increasing experience of responsibility. Once you can take care of yourself, you become able to take care of others and have others rely on you. So children should be given responsibility for themselves in the first instance.

Later, they should be expected to take some reasonable and progressive responsibility for others. This transfer is important, though the qualification 'reasonable' can be critical. For example, you might consider leaving your twelve-year-old to look after a two-year-old sibling for half an hour, but to leave them together for a whole day would not be appropriate. It would be asking too much. To have others rely on you to do something encourages 'task commitment', because there is outside pressure to carry something through. Children who are given reasonable responsibility feel trusted, competent and respected.

Independence

Self-reliance and independence are mutually reinforcing. The more self-reliant you are, the more you can manage independence. The more you experience independence, the more you build up the confidence and skills to develop self-reliance. Independence is about not depending on authority and not needing direction. If children are encouraged to get on with things themselves at home, working things out for themselves as they go along, without constant direction, they will be able to do this when they get to school and they can progress that much faster and feel more confident as a result. Parents must provide the opportunities, and time, to allow children to achieve praçtical tasks; they must be tolerant of the methods needed to achieve; and they must know how to deal with the frustration which will be inevitable.

Independence also involves the idea of being able to look after yourself and solving your own problems.

'Independence without abandonment': getting the balance right

Independence must not be foisted on children too early. Independence must not be created solely because it is convenient for the parent, with no reference to appropriateness. Sometimes, a family's practical needs are the trigger for increasing independence. But it is important to consider whether independence is being created solely as a consequence of necessity, and to be sensitive to a child's perception of your motives. An apparent *ability* to cope with the extra demands might conceal a continuing need for company, guidance and attention. The right balance to aim for is 'independence without abandonment'.

If a child feels 'put upon', 'used' or abandoned as a result of the greater responsibility and independence given to him, his self-reliance and self-esteem will be damaged, not enhanced. The independence will be counter-productive, and will cause him anguish and self-doubt which serve only to impede self-expression and confidence.

Relevant practical experience and common sense

Common sense develops through having relevant and practical experiences. Someone who is self-reliant should know, amongst other things, how to:

- feed themselves and, preferably, cook;
- take sensible decisions about spending money within a budget;
- manage public transport and crossing roads;
- use the telephone to find out information;
- react appropriately in various emergency situations.

Scope for autonomy and self-determination

Self-determination means being able to control or influence what happens to you. Children need to grow up with the experience of choices, but of limited and managed ones which they can cope with and which are unlikely to lead them into big trouble. With too much adult control, children's scope for deciding things for themselves is very limited. Where parents stand too far back and abdicate responsibility for exercising due care, children may mishandle the responsibility and control handed to them. At the same time, there will often be other aspects of the young person's life and family relationships over which they have no control.

Problem-solving skills

With appropriate support and guidance, children should be encouraged to solve their own practical and relationship problems. For example, if we are asked the common question 'What can I do, I'm bored?' instead of phoning a friend to come over every time, or playing a game with them, you can help them to write a list of things which they like to do and play – on their own or with others – (simply illustrated if they cannot read) so they can look at it in future to get ideas and take the decision themselves.

Physical competence

To be self-reliant, we also need a certain degree of strength and physical competence, and this is as true for women and girls as it is for men and boys. Sport and physical activity are important in developing or improving good co-ordination and fitness. We all know now that exercise provides us with longer-term benefits, and influences our health and general well-being. Exercise gives us renewed energy. It is thought to improve our attitude and motivation. If we are fit, we have more stamina. If it is so good for adults, and if our childhood activity levels have such a strong impact on our future health, we should make doubly sure that our children are keeping exercised and fit.

Unfortunately, research shows that our children today are getting far less exercise than they used to. In fact, some people take more notice of their dog's need for exercise than their children's. If we have a dog, we make sure they have a walk twice a day. For many of our children, their only exercise is PE once a week at school and little else, being driven most places, playing more indoors and generally leading a much more sedentary life.

Security and independence: getting the balance right

Independence is a vital and exciting part of growing up. Developing a pride in your competence;

experiencing challenges and surviving; experimenting with risks and different ways of doing things; gaining more control over what happens to you and learning to set your *own* boundaries; these are all essential if a child is to become an autonomous and responsible adult. It is vital that children have new freedoms and responsibilities, *as* and *when* they are ready to cope with them.

Unfortunately, the world outside the home is becoming an increasingly dangerous place. Parents are naturally worried about giving children greater freedom to play and travel without adult supervision. Instead of encouraging children to go off on their own and experiment, giving out rope gradually, they supervise, chaperone, constrain and contain them. Fear of traffic accidents and molestation mean children get driven or walked to school and friends' homes. They are discouraged from playing even in the front garden let alone the street or the park. Having children safely indoors, of course, frees parents from worry and gives them a wonderful feeling of relief. To add virtue to self-interest, they kid themselves that what they are doing is in the best interest of their child. But is it? Is it possible that we are losing a proper sense of balance on the issue of security versus independence? Fearful messages about 'stranger danger' could be damaging children's willingness and ability to 'go' even where the parents are happy to 'let go'.

Children and young people are now getting very mixed messages about how capable they are or ought to be. We have almost got the issue upside down. When children are small, we give them too much independence; too many choices about things which give them an inappropriate degree of responsibility and control. It gives them too much power before they are ready to manage it, when it is actually the parents' responsibility to stay in command of the controls. When children approach adolescence, however, just when they need to feel confident and be wresting some of those controls into their own hands, we tell them that it is a fearful world and, in effect, they cannot be trusted to manage themselves and cope.

The best way to acquire coping skills is through experience. Experience also builds common sense and lessens fear. If we were to drive less and walk or use public transport more, over time, children would develop road sense and a rational attitude to traffic. If we were to walk and be out and about more, children would develop a better sense of what is normal or strange behaviour, and be more confident to react in a sensible way. Confronting fears keeps them in proportion. Hiding from them makes them grow. Staying in cars or indoors is no way to acquire life skills.

The problem goes further than these practical issues. Susan Kegerreis, in a paper entitled 'Independent mobility and children's mental and emotional development' (in *Children, Transport and the Quality of Life*, ed. M. Hillman, PSI 1993), argues that:

> being able to go places on their own is extremely important in fostering children's development . . . Opportunities to be on our own are opportunities to practise, to try ourselves out . . . If we do not have such opportunities, our identity is harder to establish, self-esteem harder to build up and social adjustment – finding out how to operate in and belong to a wider society – harder to achieve.

The two main culprits are, then, the car and crime, but they are not the only things which are reducing the amount children go out on their own. The demise of the corner shop means that fewer children 'nip out' to buy groceries. Public transport is less available. With more school mergers and greater use of private schooling, children have to travel further to school. The increasing popularity of home-based entertainment, such as television, videos and video and computer games, means that children are less likely to go out or make their own creative entertainment.

Rights and responsibilities: getting the balance right

Self-reliance is about gaining independence and rights at the same time as taking on new responsibilities. If children have more responsibilities, they should also have more rights to go with them, so they can see that it is part of growing up and they are proud about it happening. If they get more rights as they get older, they should also get more responsibilities to balance out, to avoid children becoming entirely self-centred. When coupled with extra rights, and when increased at the same time as birthdays or other events acknowledging increasing maturity, responsibilities are not resented. Indeed, quite the opposite; they are accepted with pride.

Getting started
Real-world tasks:

Step One Make a list of anything you think you can give them responsibility for, e.g., brushing their teeth, getting dressed, fetching the evening paper, feeding the cat/dog, laying the table, tidying their toys or whatever task is appropriate for their age. If they are near a birthday, give them the responsibility from that date, with due preparation, so they feel a sense of pride in having the responsibility and it is seen as a natural part of growing up, not an unwelcome chore foisted upon them.

Step Two Balance the new responsibilities with rights.

Step Three	Trust them. Give them the space to do the task in and the space to make mistakes. Walk away.
Step Four	**Let go**. Gradually withdraw to increase their independence. Let them take increasing control of themselves and be involved in agreeing the new boundaries to that independence. It is essential to encourage and approve of developments towards independence, to convey the message that you trust them to be able to manage and that you approve of their lessening need for you.

Some further suggestions once you are underway

- Involve them in real-world tasks, so that they learn how to do things, such as cooking, mending things, decorating, changing plugs.
- Encourage physical activity to build up strength, co-ordination and confidence, not forgetting that girls need to be physically competent, too.
- Offer limited and achievable goals. Remember to let children progress one step at a time.
- Always reward (verbal praise is usually sufficient) even minimal achievement.
- Let them achieve the task their way.
- If they express an urge to do something, try to let it happen, as soon as possible. Respond to their spontaneity and their confidence that they can do something. Let them prove it to themselves.
- Let them define their own challenges, not those of your own making.
- Manage the mess. Have clear rules about such things as putting down protective newspaper, wearing aprons, doing certain things outdoors, where felt pens can be used. Have a plastic sheet of a size they can manage to unfold and lay in their usual play area which they are responsible for putting down if using things which can stain. Fear of 'mess' should not be allowed to stop a child's need to create and experiment.
- Let them be on their own sometimes so they

learn that they *can* entertain themselves and that being with themselves is safe and fulfilling. They are then more likely to try out new activities and adventures.

- If they have done something which pleases *them* and which they are proud of, that is good enough. *It does not matter what other people think* (unless it is school and it is something for them to evaluate).
- Warn of the potential for disappointment if their goals are unrealistic.

What are the important things to avoid?

- Never say that they are stupid if they haven't managed something.
- Don't have too high expectations.
- Don't make approval conditional on success. Trying hard, or even just having a go, is just as important.
- Don't hover over them while they are doing it. Your presence is quite likely to put them off. To walk away and leave them to it is a statement of trust, and demonstrates an assumption that it will happen.
- Beware of completing a task for them before they are finished. (Sometimes this is a practical necessity but, wherever possible, don't.) Bite back your frustration and do not convey your disappointment if they have not managed it.

Self-reliance: question check-list

- Have I given them the chance to do some real task by themselves today?
- Have I noticed, acknowledged and shown approval for any instances of independence? Or have I stamped on them because for them to do it causes me inconvenience?
- When they last had an idea about doing something which needed assistance, did I help it happen either then or later, or let it fall through a crack?

Conclusion

Children can become self-reliant only if you have encouraged their independence; given them practice in taking decisions which concern themselves; and have shown them, first, that they can be relied upon.

Three
Building a Firm Foundation: II The Repair Kit

Almost all relationships have times when they reach rock-bottom. This includes the relationship between parent and child. At these times, which may be short-lived or be much longer lasting, you may become not only depressed but also fearful either that your child will be a life-long loser, or that you cannot be an adequate parent: even, sometimes, that you are not the right person to bring up your child. Mutual trust will be low. Self-respect will be low. Patterns of behaviour and response can get established, set in motion by either of you, which make you feel that you can do nothing right. Your child's behaviour, and your responses to her at these times, are so awful that you are too embarrassed to discuss it with any of your friends. There may even be knock-on effects in her behaviour at school which you are called in to talk about. Blame and guilt will be there in quantity. The scenes which you experience within your four walls do not even appear in any of the standard child-rearing text books, so you cannot even try to work out in the privacy of your home what has gone wrong and what to do about it. Why do relationships sometimes get like this, and what tools do you need to repair the damage?

Bad times can happen for a wide variety of reasons. They rarely happen for no reason, because (as some might be tempted to think) a child has suddenly turned into a 'bad apple'. It may be that the *child* is having to cope with a stressful new experience such as the arrival of a new baby in the family, starting school, separation from someone close, or with a parent starting or changing jobs. It may be that either or both of the *parents* are having problems in their lives – for example debt, marital difficulties, the threat or reality of redundancy, or the death of someone close to them. Each of these events involves change and uncertainty. And uncertainty breeds insecurity.

If anyone within a family, parent or child, feels insecure, they will respond to things very differently: usually less consistently and less appropriately. Moods make people unpredictable. Children very quickly detect changed moods, or if a parent's mind is preoccupied with something else. They do not like things to feel different. They will seek reassurance through getting your attention and confirmation of your continuing love for them. If, after trying several times, they do not get it, they will try to protect themselves both from fear of the unfamiliar and from the pain of apparent rejection.

They protect themselves by telling themselves that they neither value their parents nor need to have their approval through trying to be co-operative or 'good', because it hurts too much when they want it and do not get it. They may even take this one step further and try to take control of events and their life by becoming uncontrollable. It will not make them happy. But at least they will not feel at the mercy of people and events which they cannot predict or understand. The problem, then, may go deeper than poor discipline. But children's response to insecurity, stress, anxiety or unhappiness frequently takes the form of challenge and disobedience. Repairing the relationship will often require a two-pronged approach dealing with both the *symptom*: poor discipline: and the *cause*: insecurity.

Power play: understanding the behaviour when there is breakdown

It may be helpful to understand and accept two things when you sit down to straighten things out. These are very important.

- When your child's behaviour is awful, try not to take it personally. Remember that she is doing it primarily to protect herself and to get attention, and because she is angry. She will not be doing it to 'get at' you. You should not need to retaliate.
- Through taking on the responsibility for putting a stop to the downward spiral, you will be able to re-establish your authority. Both parents and children feel very threatened by the loss of parental authority. The reality is that children do not want to be in control. They want, and need, the parent clearly to be in charge.

Power, authority and poor behaviour

These difficult times are usually characterised by poor behaviour, ill-discipline and a total disregard for the house rules and the needs of others. If you feel that your child is out of your control and winding you up outrageously, the chances are that, out of desperation, you will decide that you need to reassert control. Probably without much warning, you will seize the remaining power you have and start laying down the law, introducing strong punishments, or issuing threats and bribes – in other words, getting your way however you have to do it. But demonstrations of power usually produce power responses and, far from giving you good feelings of being back in the driving seat, you can end up feeling less in control than when you started. Reversing the downward spiral when both parent and child are using various power tactics is important, necessary, and not always easy. It will almost certainly require a triple strategy:

- action to draw and enforce clear boundaries to reintroduce security;
- action to improve your confidence and self-esteem;
- action to improve your child's confidence and self-esteem.

Understanding how parents and children both use, and respond to, power is an important part of the unwinding process.

Power and authority: what is the difference?

Power and authority are closely related, but they are different. That difference is important. For too long the two notions have been bundled together in parenting attitudes. The result has been that either parents feel it is within their 'rights' to use both, and the child can end up terrorised; or they reject both, leaving the child to flounder in an authority vacuum, not receiving either direction or guidance. What is the difference between power and authority? Why is it good for parents to exploit their natural *authority*, as parents, but not desirable for them to depend on using their *power*?

Authority is, of course, a form of power. It is usually understood to mean 'legitimate' power, or 'accepted' power. Power can be 'accepted' in two senses. Firstly, in relation to **the person who has power**. Is it right that a particular person has power – the ability to control the behaviour of others – in a particular circumstance? Democratically elected political leaders have power; we accept that. Having won elections, they have a right to make decisions – sometimes ones we do not like – on our behalf. Secondly, in relation to **how they use that power**. Do they use their power in a way in which most people would agree was acceptable? For example, most people in democracies would agree that it is acceptable for politicians to take decisions about taxes, but not ones which concern what colour car we drive, or whether we can travel outside our country.

There are several circumstances in which people broadly agree that it is acceptable for someone to have both authority and the implied access to the means to enforce that authority (the tools of power) if that is the only way to exercise it. One situation, just mentioned, is where people have been *elected* to the position of authority – *political* authority. Another is where someone *traditionally* and *legally* has authority in that role, such as a parent, or a teacher. A third is where someone seems to command authority because of their personality, and naturally takes control when it is helpful for someone to take either the lead or the responsibility.

Parental authority

This book is concerned, of course, with parental authority. But looking at other examples of authority can help to illustrate the difference between power and authority. Authority, then, does not always involve taking decisions about how others should behave in the sense of purely exercising control over them. It is also about taking the lead, offering guidance and, above all, accepting responsibility. People in authority take responsibility for others. They have to be sensitive to the needs of the whole community they manage, and operate in a way which delivers the greatest good to the greatest number. They cannot give in to one group exclusively at the expense of another. This is very similar to the role which should be taken by the parent within the family.

Ideally, if someone has authority, or is in a position of authority, there should be little need to enforce the authority using the tools of power which are available. But we do not live in an ideal world. Children do challenge, will challenge, and even need to challenge. It is a very rare child, and a not very well-rounded one, who does everything she is told. So there will often be times when we will have to back up our authority and enforce our decisions. In other words, we resort to power when our authority does not 'work', and use techniques other than merely asking to *make* people do what we want. These techniques can be called **the tools of power**. Provided the techniques we use are both fair and reasonable, and keep within the boundaries of what would be considered 'acceptable' – which means, broadly, that they meet the requirement that 'the punishment fit the crime' and they are not designed to humiliate – we will not be either abusing our power or using illegitimate power. But resorting to power too often, even if it is not over-strict, can cause resentment and can lead to the disintegration of the relationship. First, we will look in more detail at the tools of power which both parents and children have at their disposal. Second, ways to re-establish and support parental authority will be considered.

How parents use power

Parents have both power and authority. Of course they have power; they are physically stronger; they are better at using words to get their way; for a significant number of years, they control the child's access to money, food, mobility, entertainment and independence, things which children either need or desire; and, psychologically, most parents will need the child less than the child needs the parents. It is a profoundly unequal relationship and the scope for abuse is vast.

Many of the problems which parents have in keeping an organised and calm home stem, as has already been mentioned, from people believing that power and authority are the same thing. 'Liberal' or 'permissive' parents who reject the available tools of parental power can end up throwing out their authority at the same time. In striving to be 'equal', they can fail to give the vital lead which every child needs, and fail to take the responsibility for their child as she grows up. At the other end of the spectrum, 'authoritarian' parents, who feel that they must always be 'in authority' and in command, can believe that it is quite acceptable regularly to use the tools of power to maintain and reinforce this position.

The tools of power

Power is a reality of life. It is a feature, hidden or otherwise, of most relationships. Power does not only involve physical force. People also use emotional and verbal techniques to get their way. Parents may believe that because they do not hit or physically damage their children they are not using power. They would be mistaken. Children are sensitive to all the tools of power used by adults.

The tools of power used by parents include:

Physical
- hitting
- hurting
- damaging belongings

Verbal
- bribery
- ridicule

Emotional
- threats
- sarcasm
- shouting
- withdrawal
- witholding food, liberty, etc.

How children use power

Despite their physical inferiority, children very quickly learn to identify the tools of power available to them. Power is not just about having control. It is also being able to *take* control when you want to. Children have many devices at their disposal to take control.

Defensive or attention-seeking behaviour takes the form of:

- disruption: breaking the flow, the silence
- challenge: testing the boundaries and your reactions
- crying/whingeing/whining/moaning
- refusing to acknowledge you or what you say
- damaging your property, or a sibling's toys
- damaging things in their bedroom
- walking out of the house
- refusing to talk to or answer questions, particularly when cornered
- being verbally and physically abusive to you or to other family members
- food or clothes fads

These tools of power are used when parent and child are desperate. They are the responses of someone trying to keep one step ahead; trying to pay the other back for the last challenge or humiliation, tit-for-tat style. They are not usually rational. They are almost always inappropriate and unreasonable.

They are inappropriate for two reasons. First, because they escalate quickly and soon lose any relationship to the scale of the issue at hand. We can find ourselves saying and doing the most outrageous things when the initial fight was over something quite petty. Second, and far more important, because they do not work. **They solve nothing**. When the fight spirals out of control, then is the time to take stock and agree a plan of action.

Getting started

Step One — ***Repair your own self-esteem***. Do something that you enjoy doing, that you are good at, something which you used to take pride in being good at (see Chapter Four).

Step Two — ***Make the first move and take responsibility***. Don't wait for the child to make it better. She is only a child. You are the adult and you must take the responsibility for bringing about change. Take the responsibility for the state of the relationship away from her. She will not understand why the relationship has changed and become difficult and will almost certainly be feeling some guilt. Be open about the difficult time you are both having, and avoid blaming and thus stereotyping her and creating the self-fulfilling prophecy. Instead, you can say something like, *'I know that you haven't been yourself lately. I have been pretty horrible too.'* She will not have been feeling happy or proud about how she has been behaving.

Step Three — ***Make the second, third and fourth moves.*** Don't expect a quick change or immediate reciprocation from her. Don't make your next moves dependent on her responding with better behaviour straight away. After a bad patch, trust is thin. You have to keep it going. TRY to keep cool, not to lose your temper and shout.

Step Four — ***Rebuild the structure and routines of your family*** which are likely to have been destroyed by challenges and ill-discipline. Set out clear rules and clear routines, to reintroduce security and predictability. Announce the new rules clearly, and do not debate them. Explain them, and make sure they are not presented as a form of punishment. Choose one or two things to implement and enforce at the beginning – select, perhaps, one time of day and get the new patterns established there before going on to regulate other times. Alternatively, start with the time of day which gets you down most – bedtime or getting ready for school. Keep it simple and manageable. Make sure that your rules are *clear and fair, simple to understand and implement*, and *reasonable*. And keep critical comments on her behaviour in other areas to a minimum.

Step Five ***Praise her and her good behaviour as much as you can***, while you are working on getting her to keep to these new rules, to make her feel loved, lovable and wanted. For some reason we find it much easier to be negative than positive. Provided you are honest about the bad or disruptive things she does, you cannot praise too much. At the same time, try as hard as you can to ignore minor incidents of bad behaviour. Frequent nagging and telling off will only send messages of failure and disapproval. She may then lose the urge to try to get your pleasure and approval by doing what you ask on the priority things you have selected. High expectations that she will be able to change her behaviour and be sensible and co-operative will show that you trust her and are more likely to produce the results that you want.

Step Six ***Develop her self-esteem and confidence***. Help her to feel better about herself and give her a positive self-image. Put into practice 'The Expertise' (see Chapter Five).

Some further suggestions once you are underway

A human relationship is a very special, complex

and finely balanced thing. When it is badly fractured, like a shattered antique vase, repairing it can require skill and patience.

Repairing a relationship involves:

- touching the child
- spending time with and enjoying her
- being firm and clear, but friendly and loving
- praising and approving her and what she does and cutting down on criticism
- avoiding the use of questions
- offering a few limited and managed choices

Using touch

Touch is a very powerful tool, with the potential to either heal or hurt. Although touching is usually done silently, it is also a very powerful way to communicate. There is a whole language associated with touch. Provided the contact is not designed to hurt, children love – indeed yearn – to be touched. However, a child who feels hurt, rejected and resentful is very likely to reject the first overtures of touch. He might push you away, or get up and walk away. If he does, do not give up. Remember – do not make conciliation dependent on reciprocation. It takes time to rebuild trust, so the trick is to be subtle and even devious about it; to find ways to get physically close which do not involve a big statement and which do not require him to return the gesture. In other words, it is best to start with **'giving' touches** and not with **'giving and taking'** or **reciprocated touches**.

Examples of **two-way, 'giving and taking' touches** are body embraces, holding hands, walking arm in arm, even shaking hands.

Examples of **one-way, 'giving' touches** include:

- sitting beside them while they watch television;
- casual body touches as a welcome when you

see them after an absence, e.g., after school;

- sitting next to them in the car, if changing the regular pattern does not seem too strange;
- sharing a bath if they are of an appropriate age;
- sitting or lying on their bed next to them at bedtime.

Never reject their touch or physical demonstrations of affection – even if they have just been diabolical. If they have made you angry, tell them in words what it is they have done which you did not like. Rejecting their physical advances will convey that it is them, and not their behaviour, that you dislike. Rejecting their physical gestures of need and apology – a complex mix of emotions which it will be impossible for them to express in words – will erect yet another protective barrier and make the reconciliation harder to achieve and even further away.

If *they* give *you* a 'giving' touch, **make sure you reciprocate**. Accept their olive branch, if that is what it is, and acknowledge and meet their need for you and your approval.

Time with them and for them

When the relationship is fractured, at the beginning the time you spend with and for the child must be on his terms. This won't always be easy. Young children need to play. It has been said that children use play much as adults use clothes – as the outward expression of their inner selves. Playing what they want to play means that you accept them as they are. But parents do not always find it easy to play. Although most of us played in our own childhood, we often forget how to do it, or feel uncomfortable doing it. Take the lead from your child. Talk to him about what he is doing. Do not take it over.

Older children 'play' in different ways. They do not play with dolls or cars or building bricks anymore. Perhaps the best way to re-establish communication with an older child is to sit with him while he watches his favourite television programme, watch him play football in the park, or ask him to show you how he does whatever it is he takes pride in. Again, it must start by being on his terms, doing things which he likes to do. If you have already listed the likes and dislikes of your child as was suggested earlier, you should be able to identify the point from which, gently, to build bridges.

Beware sabotage!

Like touch, giving your time must be done sensitively. We can apply the same idea of 'one-way' and 'two-way' touching to time. Giving time on your child's terms and asking for nothing in return is a **'one-way' time gift**. Reciprocal, or **'two-way'** giving of time, is inviting him to do something with you which you like to do, in which he has to actively participate with you.

Where there have been many arguments and many disappointments, there will inevitably be mistrust. If you create expectations for your time together which are too high, and if you make your child take equal or more responsibility for making a success of the time, there is a chance that he will sabotage it, refuse to co-operate and *make* it fail, to protect himself against the disappointment of it possibly ending in breakdown as on previous occasions. Saying something like: *'I think we need to spend some happy time together. I have arranged for your sister to visit a friend so that we can be alone. What would you like to do?'* puts enormous pressure on the child to keep things calm. He may respond by saying he wants to do something which does not involve you – thus defeating the objective – or he may quickly engineer a row to end the uncertainty – thus avoiding the responsibility. If you recognise the pattern, be patient. It is common and understandable. You have to begin again by offering **'one-way' time and attention** to demonstrate your commitment, because his trust in you being there for him has been undermined.

Examples of **one-way time** for your child, time which does not require him to do anything in return are:

- read to him;
- watch him as he is doing what he enjoys or is good at, e.g., sports, tree-climbing;
- do things in parallel, so talking is not necessary and nothing is at stake. Do your chores in the same room where he is doing something else, provided it is not his bedroom. Conversely, you could invite him to join you and keep you company.

Be firm and clear, but friendly and loving

Make statements. Keep them short. If you use explanations, use as few as possible – if one will do, just use that and say nothing more. Don't use 'floppy' phrases such as 'I think', 'perhaps', 'maybe'. 'Please' is friendly, but sometimes gets the answer 'no'. Use it carefully.

State clearly what it is that you want to happen: '*I am letting you know now that when we go to the shops today, I shall not be buying you any sweets or toys. This is a shopping expedition for our food, not for anything else.*' And stick to it. It means that you have to think ahead about the problems which may arise, and build a plan. But it will be time well invested.

Continue to give plenty of praise and approval

Say you like what he does, you like who he is, and you like being with him.

Avoid unnecessary questions

Questions need answers. They are best avoided, because both questions, and the answers to them, can be used inappropriately as tools of power.

Using questions as power Questions need answers and demand attention. They can therefore be intrusive and put people on the defensive. Adults frequently use questions to control children, to seek information children might not want to give, and to get information on *their* terms. Too many questions can cause resentment. Always use the 'Need to Know Test'. Ask yourself before you speak: do I really *need* to know that?

Snooping questions Children should be allowed autonomy: some space in their lives in which they are accountable only to themselves. This is particularly true of their thoughts. Although it is sometimes fascinating to know what is going on in their heads, much of the time that is nobody's business but theirs. They have to be allowed to grow in their own way. Asking too many snooping questions will serve only to inhibit growth by making them feel untrustworthy.

Trip-wire questions Asking a question to which you already know the answer is a power tactic which can cause enormous resentment, especially if your prior knowledge is discovered. If you know the answer, do not ask the question. Instead of '*What have you been doing here?*' you can say '*I can see that you have been drawing on your brother's book!*' Using questions to catch them out is also unhelpful because they will feel manipulated.

Put-down questions Parents often use questions to which they do not really expect an answer, to 'rub their child's nose' in a failure. For example, '*Why are you so stupid?*' or '*Why are you so clumsy?*' are both much more demeaning than '*That was a clumsy/stupid thing to do.*'

Using answers as power Asking a question immediately hands the initiative to the person who is going to answer. It puts them centre-stage and potentially gives them enormous scope to choose between compliance or disruption, to set or change the agenda.

- Asking a question gives the idea that there is a choice of action when there is none. *'Shall we go up to bed now?'* is probably not what you really mean!
- Out of the choices which are available, you might get the answer you realise only then that you *really* did not want.
- Asking questions and giving choices sometimes gives the impression that you are unclear about what should be happening. That is why you are asking. Remember, don't be floppy.
- Being given the chance to answer is an invitation to the child to offer a challenge and say he wants the opposite. It allows him to retake control.
- A child who is feeling insecure will want the parent to be decisive, to take the responsibility and not to pass it over. Answers require the respondent to make a statement, to make a stand and be clear about things. The child is not always ready for that. Questions such as *'Are you feeling fed up today?'* are discomforting. He will not know which is the best answer to give, tactically or otherwise. It might lead to another question, *'Why?'*, which he almost certainly will wish to avoid. If, instead, you use a statement such as *'I can see that today you are feeling fed up about something'*, it allows him to continue feeling fed up, and be relieved that you have understood.

Choices

Limited and managed choices give the opportunity for autonomy. If your child has been trying to take control, then he may feel resentful and fearful about all his control being taken away at once. Giving him limited opportunities to decide things for himself will help not only to offset any feelings of fear or even panic that he has lost control, but also to take some responsibility for himself and to establish a picture of who he is. Choices about things which are particularly personal, for example what clothes to wear or how to spend his time, are therefore most appropriate at the beginning. As he becomes more accommodating and trustworthy, the scope for choice can be extended.

Giving choices involves asking questions and seems, therefore, to go against the advice offered in the previous section. The emphasis must be on both **limited** and **managed** choices.

Managed choice means that you decide what options your child is given to choose between, making sure that you will be happy with which ever choice he makes. For example, on a cold day you may ask: *'Would you like to wear your track suit or jeans and a jumper?'* instead of the open question *'What would you like to wear today?'* which might produce an unsuitable answer. If that degree of choice leads to confrontation, it maybe appropriate to offer only a choice of socks: *'Would you like the blue or the red socks today?'*

Limited choice means you keep the opportunities for even managed choice to a few times a day. As his behaviour stabilises and his sense of security increases, the number of choices can be increased. It will be important gradually to extend the choices, for children as well as adults need to develop a sense of autonomy and have some scope for self-determination.

Managing deadlock and defiance:

Achieving agreement and compliance without playing power

Management training for people in senior positions as leaders or negotiators contains a great deal of advice on how to reach agreement in ways which keep all the people involved happy. Much of this advice can be applied to the relationship between parent and child. There is, however, an important difference between the two situations. In many areas of **management**, the other party has a right to reject the solution or walk away from it if it does not suit them. Solutions cannot be imposed. The aim, therefore, is to reach **agreement**. For **parents**, the objective is to achieve **compliance**. Agreement is desirable but not necessary. Ultimately, we can and often do require that children meet our demands whether they like them or not. We are in a position of power, and we have the ultimate deterrent of positive sanctions (e.g., bribes or other rewards) and negative sanctions (e.g., punishments) available to get our way. However, the aim must always be to get compliance using our authority and other methods before we have to resort to sanctions which are the tools of power.

Despite this difference, there is a lot to learn from the techniques and analyses offered to managers. After all, we are looking at the same kind of skills – **people skills**. As has been discussed earlier in this chapter, power solutions should be used as little as possible because they establish unhelpful, tit-for-tat style practices and patterns; they pass on bad habits and unhelpful social skills to children; and they generally end up damaging the parent-child relationship. So what are the key ways of achieving compliance? How can we best manage our children to minimise the amount of conflict and negative power play and maximise the positive experiences of parenting?

There are four basic ways to get compliance. These are through:

- trust
- reason
- creativity
- power and sanctions

Trust

A child who feels trusted by an adult tends to feel proud of that trust. She therefore likes to live up to the expectations that adult has of her to strengthen it. All the research on human behaviour shows that high expectations of performance produce good results, and low expectations produce poor results. We can use a computer term in current vogue to illustrate this. 'Wysiwyg' (pronounced 'wizzywig') is the jargon shorthand for the common phrase, 'What you see is what you get'. 'What you see', in this case, is your perception of your child's personality and behaviour. 'What you get' is the behaviour you expect. It is another way of describing the self-fulfilling prophecy. So, if you ask a child to do things in a way which assumes and expects that she will, you are more likely to have her comply. The same is true with the reverse – when you let slip that you think she will not do as you want.

For example, *'Time for school in ten minutes. Remember what you need and I'll see you at the front door at quarter to'* is better than *'You've only got ten minutes. Have you got your homework, have you done your teeth, don't forget your games kit, and don't be late like yesterday!'*

Without realising it, we often use forms of words which undermine the trust, which show that we are actually not sure that a child will be able to carry out what we ask. Above is an elaborate example. More often, we just slip in the one-word question, 'Promise?', and pop goes the trust.

Seeking a promise to back up the commitment to deliver undermines your child's belief in your trust, it destroys the expectation that, naturally, she will be able to achieve what you have asked and, of itself, plants the idea of non-compliance. It may even be seen as a challenge and could spur defiance. This is the most common way the 'trust' strategy can backfire. Another is that the expectations you have may be too ambitious. A promise or expectation that is hard to deliver *sets the child up to fail*. Make sure, then, that the expectation is realistic and age-appropriate.

What happens if you show trust, keep your expectations sensible, but your child still fails to deliver? For example, she is still not getting up early enough to avoid last-minute panic before school, continues to forget her homework or swimming kit, her clothes still lie in piles over the bedroom floor? What can you do then? Should you start nagging and reminding again? **No**.

Before you return to that you could:

- **put her further in charge** and give her *more* responsibility. For example, give her an alarm clock so you do not have to wake her up; give her peel-off notepads which she can use to remind herself;
- **let her 'face the music'**, be late, leave things behind, go to school in her pyjamas (yes, this is what one mother did at the teacher's suggestion and the child never refused to get dressed again!), leave homework undone – learning the hard way is often foolish, but sometimes it is the most effective way;
- **work out a system or routine together** which will help her to remember tasks and responsibilities.

Note: If you trust, and expect compliance, and your child in turn trusts you to behave fairly and broadly in her interests, this amounts to you **exercising your authority** and her accepting it.

Reason

Getting agreement or compliance using reason is highly desirable. Rather than merely issuing decrees and demanding that your will be done, like a dictator, this strategy involves giving reasons for asking the child to do particular things. The request is therefore seen as reasonable and sensible, and its and your purpose is understood. Giving reasons not only teaches children to be rational – that it is appropriate to be able and willing to account for behaviour, and to recognise what constitute strong and weak reasons – but it also shows that you respect their right to know.

The tendency to treat children as people with rights, interests and feelings is the great advance in child-rearing in the latter half of this century. This lies at the heart of the child-centred approach championed by the famous child psychologists of the sixties and seventies and which is now being called into question by people who wish to turn the clock back and 'bring back discipline'. It may seem difficult to understand how this eminently civilised approach to the parent-child relationship can go wrong. But it can. And it largely has. It is important to understand why it does not always work, so that its misapplication can be corrected and the vital elements of it can be retained and not thrown out in any pendulum swing back to the Victorian idea of children being seen but not heard.

What can go wrong? The problem is that too much emphasis on reason can lead to *too much talk* which can obscure, manipulate and *confuse rather than* *clarify*. Young children, especially, cannot cope with complex argument and logic. Words can be used to entangle and manipulate and can very easily become tools of power. Every child under the age of, say, ten will be at a disadvantage with just about every adult when it comes to a verbal competition. Once power is seen as the name of the game, children will dig in their heels, using their own power tactics, and clashes will inevitably follow.

Explanation or persuasion? Even with older children, the 'rational' approach can misfire. If more than one or two reasons are given to explain a request, they not only open the door to counter arguments, but also can appear as attempts to *persuade* the child – which automatically gives him the opportunity to remain unpersuaded. Persuasion implies a right of veto. And what if he says no?

Keep the boundaries clear First and foremost, it is important to keep the boundaries – the rules and requirements – clear. If reason gets the upper hand, and you listen and accommodate too much to counter-reasons, the boundaries are likely to be adjusted and qualified so much that children never really know where they stand or what is expected of them.

How to cut down on the 'verbals'

- State your reasons briefly and firmly. Use only one or two strong arguments, even if there are more. Then stay quiet and wait, expectantly.
- Give reasons the child will understand.
- Beware justifying the reasons further. Think (but don't say!): do I *really* need to justify myself to a ... year-old?
- Use silence, facial expression and *gentle* and directive touch more. A gentle ushering, hands on shoulders, in the direction of the bedroom can say a final 'Upstairs now' more convincingly than the words repeated yet again.

Note: If you give *one or two reasons only* as explanation, rather than persuasion or justification, you are **in effect exercising your authority** – rationally and not dictatorially. You are saying, gently: this is what I expect, this is why, now go and do it.

Creativity

Creative solutions to deadlock and defiance defuse or divert attention from the (usually quite petty) issue at hand, allowing parent, child, or both to get things back in proportion and climb down without loss of face. Both sides can get caught in a battle of wills in which the potential damage to the relationship far outweighs the importance of the matter in dispute. Try to remember that **you are the adult** – which should *not* be interpreted as giving you the right to win – which means that you have both the ability to keep the issue in perspective, to look beyond the moment, *and* the responsibility and maturity to know when enough is enough and to bring it to an end.

Tactics for defusing deadlock include:

- changing the subject
- making things fun
- compromise
- humour

Changing the subject We are all capable of getting wound up about things, when we force an issue, find arguments to use for argument's sake, and take the issue much further than we ever intended. Children do the same. When your child is winding you up, perhaps just to get your attention, it is far better to ignore it and talk about something completely different, or suggest doing something together to get the issue dropped. Trying to 'win' the argument, or rising to the challenge of a minor insult, will only stir up trouble. Showing that you are unmoved by his challenges may even mean that he eventually gives them up.

Making things fun Car journeys, shopping trips, and collecting brothers and sisters from school, can be made fun. For example, on any walk you can count how many front doors of different colours or cats and dogs that you pass. You can count how many manhole covers you see. Car journeys can be made livelier by collecting pub names or makes of car.

Compromise Compromise is a situation in which both parties get something (the important bits) of what they want but not all of it. It is therefore a 'win-win' outcome. Compromise is a gesture of strength, not of weakness. Provided it creates an alternative which genuinely meets everyone's interests, and is not a disguise for a climbdown by the parent, it is a creative way out of, or to avoid, deadlock. It shows respect for the interests of the child, will enhance his self-esteem, and will give him problem-solving skills which he can use immediately to his advantage when playing with brothers and sisters or with friends at home and at school. (See Chapter Five, 'The Expertise'.)

Humour See the funny side of the often ridiculous situation you are both caught up in. Laugh at yourself, or gently at both of you – but never at them alone! Laughter and humour are great natural remedies; great tools for releasing tension.

How can this strategy go wrong? Creative solutions can also backfire unless carefully deployed. Children sometimes need to do what they are told, and quickly, especially if their safety is threatened. If they are frequently allowed to wriggle their way out of a straight demand, one day they might find themselves facing danger. Another problem is that they can learn and adopt the same techniques and not always use them at the right times. They can certainly exhaust you with their ingenuity when the last thing you feel like is a long-winded discussion of all the alternatives.

Children can, therefore, get wise to your game because, like reasons, compromises can be manipulative. For a while, you will always have better ideas than they will. Make sure that *their* creativity is not manipulation, a version of power play, expressing a need always to retain some control of events.

While compromise (win-win) is desirable, climb-down (win-lose) is not. Beware of dressing up your capitulation as compromise to make it seem acceptable. A rough guide to tell which you are doing might be how soon the 'compromise' option develops. The sooner you hit upon it, the more genuine it will be. The later it appears, the more potential there is for manipulation and giving in.

What can you do if your child finds straight demands difficult? To be able to argue, to make critical judgements and to identify concessions are very valuable skills for children to develop. Just as important, though, is the sense to recognise when these responses are not appropriate – when it is simplest and best to accept the boundary where it is and not to start the negotiation process. Parents can help their children to develop this by:

- **Compromising less**. It is sensible to be flexible on the issues about which a child feels strongly, such as being able to do her favourite activity. However, on lesser or unimportant issues it will be wise to stick to what was previously agreed or to insist that what *you* want to happen takes place.

- **Acknowledge the child's interests and feelings** even if you are not taking them into account this time. His resentment at being overridden will be lessened if he feels that you know and understand how he is feeling and why he is reacting that way to your demand.

Power and the use of sanctions (punishments and rewards)

Parents can always try to impose their will by using their power and authority. Sometimes this is appropriate, but sometimes it is not. We have to find the right balance between staying 'in charge', but not getting caught up in power battles to prove it.

The key thing is to use our authority sparingly, concentrating on the important issues such as children's safety and behaving decently to others – us included. If we get into the habit of controlling many areas of their lives through power, either using punishments, shouting or threats and bribes, the strategy is very likely to backfire. We may end up losing our power, our authority and our self-respect as well.

How can this strategy go wrong?

- We may not realise that things like threats and bribes, or shouting and shaming, are forms of power which children grow to resent deeply.
- We may not appreciate that power tactics are often a *challenge* to misbehaviour because it allows the child to stay in control.
- If power tactics are used too often they become easier to ignore and invite power responses.

Relying on power, either physical or emotional, is counter-productive. It is temporary because there comes a time when power runs out; and it is, usually, emotionally damaging to the child.

How can you unravel the tangle if it does go wrong? When you find yourself in constant power battles, you must change the ground rules for the relationship. Stop using the tools of power and instead rely on your parental authority.

- Try getting compliance through using **trust, reason, creativity** and **understanding**.
- It will be important to **reduce the number of fights**. Choose one or two negative behaviours to work on at a time.
- Try to **stop shouting** and issuing threats and conditions. Try what some people call the 'soft no'. Instead of getting louder and louder, the demand should be said quieter and quieter, looking the child in the eye as you say it.
- If you mean business, you must **use the right body language**. This means standing face to face with the child; stopping what else you are doing while you say no; and staying still while you wait for him to carry out the demand.
- Sometimes, you need to **gently direct** him – lift him out of the bath, usher him to his bedroom, or in through the front door.
- Give him **choices** to help him feel back in control of his own life.
- **Spend time** with your child to help him realise that you care.

(See also 'Getting started', page 65.)

Four
Where Do You Fit In?

At the same time as looking after our children, we have to look after ourselves. If we don't, the job of bringing up children will be much less enjoyable and therefore harder than it need be. We have to start with learning to be comfortable and happy with ourselves. We have to understand our own need for play, praise, love and growth, go at least some way to meeting those needs, and learn to accept ourselves as we are. Only then can we freely and unthreateningly love our children, and accept *them* as *they* are. Children, and even small babies, must always be seen as whole people, just like ourselves. If we can learn to be more aware of ourselves and what makes us feel good or perform at our best, that is the most important route to understanding our children and getting the best out of them.

No human being is sufficiently saintly to be able to think about someone else's interests all the time to the exclusion of their own. Nor should this even be thought of as a desirable state of affairs. Children demand and need a great deal of time and attention. Giving as much as they sometimes want takes a lot out of you. Indeed, they can take so much out that you can often wonder whether there is anything left of you. If you do not consciously take the time regularly to replenish yourself, to recharge your batteries, in other words, to take time out for you and to develop your own self-esteem, you can find yourself putting up protective barriers around yourself in a desperate and arbitrary way. You may be holding on to yourself, but you might also be cutting yourself off from your child when, or especially when, your child needs you most and you feel most drained.

The best way to help your children grow up happy and healthy is to make sure that you also go on growing throughout this process and that there is something in it for you. That doesn't always happen smoothly or quite to plan. What you are able to do with or for one child, you won't be able to do for the next. All of this is inevitable.

The most sensible thing to do about this is to accept from the beginning that you must make space in your life for you. 'Pie in the sky!' I hear lots of you say. It needn't be. The important thing is not to go for too much at the wrong time. Of course, we all know that the most trying times for anyone with small children is when it is hardest to get away – when your baby is small and if you are breast-feeding; when your children are under three and too young to go to any playgroup. But at those times, even a very short break doing something that you like doing, that corresponds with your image of yourself or makes you feel good and indulged can make the world of difference. What all mums need is a bit of 'respite' care!

You need to work on your own self-esteem at the same time as working on your child's. You need to continue to consider your own personal growth while you help your child to grow. You can't put yourself into cold storage or on to the back burner for the duration. Why? Very simply because:

- when you are feeling good, you are nicer to everyone around you;
- when you become aware of what makes you feel good, and how good you can feel when things are going right for you, it gives you a much better insight into how to help your child to feel the same way;
- the more there is in your life, the more you can demonstrate to your child by example how much there is 'out there' to enjoy – they may even take an interest in, and so share, what so obviously interests you;
- the more there is in your life, the less you are there as a door mat for everyone else's convenience and the more you are able to teach them to respect other people's needs, space and general personal boundaries.

What is your little luxury? What makes you feel good?

- When others tell you that you look good?
- Reading a good trashy book?
- Going to the pictures?
- Reading a newspaper or magazine?
- Going to the shops, and buying something, small (tights or hairband) or large (beware!).
- Having a long, scented or foamy bath, uninterrupted.
- Going for a walk in the park at *your* pace, and not having to talk to a single child?
- When your partner comes and gives you a large and spontaneous hug?
- Sitting and having a cup of tea and a gossip with your best friend?
- Going out on your own to town, just to walk around and see other 'grown-up' people leading 'normal' lives?

- Having a pub lunch with your partner or friend?

For each person, the chosen thing will be different, precisely because you are unique. What you choose defines who you are. It's entirely up to you to decide. No-one else can, or should, do it for you. And the fact that you make a choice also gives you a sense of being in control of your life. It would be hard to under-estimate the beneficial effect of feeling that you are, once again, in control of yourself.

What's the pattern?

Instead of seeing your choices about how you would like to spend a free afternoon as a series of one-off, unconnected episodes, you may find it useful to see if they conform to a pattern. If they do, then you can begin to think of other things to do which, for example, may take less time or money and be easier to set up.

- Do you like to end up with something to talk about, a topic of conversation other than babies, to help you appear more interesting to your partner or socially confident with others?
- Is it praise from a special, or any, source which gives you the lift?
- Is it doing something on your own, making you realise you can still survive in the big wide world out there?
- Is it other adult company, uninterrupted by a little person's toilet needs and pestering, which you crave?
- Is it doing something energetic or physical which revitalises you – doing 'keep fit', playing tennis, going for a swim or a run?
- Do you only feel really good when others say nice things about you? (A reality, but it can be dangerous!) Try to be more in control of *when* it happens!

Seeing a pattern also helps you to be aware of the kind of person you are, making it easier to reassert your identity.

Beware!

- ***Choose something achievable***. Grandiose schemes, unless very well organised, are often doomed to fail and this will have the opposite of the desired effect!
- ***Don't put it off because there is not enough time***. Write down, say, four or six different time periods – 5 minutes, 15 minutes, one hour, two hours, half a day, a whole day, covering what realistically may be available to you – and write in what you could or would like to do in each of them. When one of the time holes opens up, fill it with the task or activity appropriate to it, e.g., 'I've got ten minutes spare. That's my time slot for putting some make-up on/ reading the front page of the newspaper . . .'
- ***If possible, set it up to happen on a regular basis***. This might mean organising a childminding swap with a friend, asking your mother to come over and babysit, or getting the children in the bath five minutes early. While some things which make you feel good can be slotted into small time slots which just appear, others need longer time and therefore need to be planned for.
- ***Don't choose something which acts counter to any other goal or requirement in your life*** because it will then have little long-term benefit and will only make you feel guilty or a failure later. For example, don't choose going out to have a coffee and cake with a friend if you are always trying to lose weight. Don't choose going out and spending money on yourself if you usually have to live within a tight budget.
- ***You may feel that you would want to choose to do something with your partner***. However, if the exercise is designed to help you get a clear picture of who *you* are and what makes *you* feel good, it is

probably advisable to pick on at least one thing to do which has nothing to do with a regular partner.

'I've always wanted to . . .'

So do it! Go for it!

But who *am* I?

If you can't think of anything to do which says something significant about you and which you are happy to identify with, think back to the things you used to enjoy doing in 'life before children'. Although as time goes by the new experiences we have mean that we change and develop, those same experiences can cause us, sometimes, to leave a part of ourselves behind. See if it is possible to resurrect old interests and rediscover that buried, but not lost, identity.

How can I help my child to be strong and confident if I'm so unsure about myself?

It is sometimes said that if a parent does not have self-esteem, she cannot give it to her child. This defeatist or negative statement makes one important mistake. It assumes that self-esteem exists as a constant quantity which exists throughout the whole of one's life, instead of seeing it as something which fluctuates and changes, something which can be topped up or drawn down. It rather assumes that either you have it or you don't. And that if you have it, you have it in a set quantity which is constant.

Life is not like that. We all have our times when we feel stronger and more confident, and times when we feel less able to cope or feel we have nothing to offer. When we are feeling good about ourselves, we are less vulnerable to other people's criticism, but we are not immune to being undermined if the criticism is continuous, is from a particularly valued person or is particularly cruel. Self-esteem can, therefore, be undermined or boosted. There is little point in trying to work out, if indeed that is possible, how much self-esteem you or your child has. There are, of course, no appropriate units of measurement. The key point is that in virtually every situation we experience, someone else can make quite a difference to how good or bad we feel about ourselves. And how we feel about ourselves, to repeat the key message of this book, influences significantly how we behave towards and interact with other people. As adults, we also have the ability, to an extent, to control it ourselves. Not only should we have a better idea of what does give us a boost, we also are in a much better position to make it happen. We are much more in charge of our own time. The responsibility for breaking out of any downward spiral lies with us. It is up to us, the adult, to lift both ourselves and our children to a point where we no longer need to taunt or deflate them, or 'put them down', in order to protect ourselves.

Five
A Way to Remember the Key Points: 'The Expertise'

What is the 'Expertise'?

'The Expertise' is not something which only the 'experts' or 'professionals' have. It is, instead, something which you have within you, within your grasp. From the beginning, this book has tried to persuade parents to trust themselves, to pay attention to who they are and to do it their way. *You* are the expert about you and your child. 'The Expertise' is, instead, really a collection of tools for the job – a technique both for remembering the key points to help you decide what to do in any particular situation *and* a guide for what you need to do for yourself to keep you sane and help you to develop yourself.

Each tool relates to a syllable, individual letter or pair of letters in the word 'Expertise', as follows:

EXPERTISE	**Ex**plain, **Ex**ample
EX**P**ERTISE	**P**raise, **P**eace, **P**lay
EXPER**T**ISE	**T**rust, **T**ouch, **T**ime, **T**alk
EXPERT**ISE**	Empath**ise**, Sympath**ise**, Apolog**ise**, Comprom**ise**

Each of these 'tools' will be discussed in turn; and

each discussion covers both how to use this tool to help *your child*, and how to apply it to *yourself*, to boost your own self-esteem. Looking after yourself, as we have already seen, will not only make you feel better. It will also help you to appreciate how *effective* these key concepts are for improving self-image, and make you more *committed* to applying them to your child.

EXplain; EXample

*EX*PLAIN

If you explain things to your child you show that you:

- respect her *right to know*
- empathise with her *need to make sense* of her immediate world
- respect her *ability to comprehend and understand*
- *trust* her

One of the most important needs we all have is to be kept informed about things which affect us. We get extremely annoyed if employers, partners, schools or neighbours do things which affect our lives without consulting us or, at the very least, warning us. Children, of course, have less experience of life and people to help them to anticipate what might happen or what might be the consequences of certain events. They will therefore feel *more* confused, uncertain and insecure than adults would if they are not told when, why or for how long things will be different. If you do not give your children explanations, they will suffer.

- **They will live in an environment which seems arbitrary**. They will be unable, therefore, to predict anything about their life and cannot possibly develop any sense of security in their relations with the outside world. They will feel vulnerable and will work out ways to protect themselves from the discomfort of uncertainty. They may *withdraw, learn to control others,* which is the closest they can get to controlling their circumstances, or *control themselves* by developing rigid, inflexible patterns for their own behaviour.

- **They will find it difficult to get a sense of their own worth.** It will be difficult for them to believe themselves to be important if no-one else bothers to keep them informed of changes, events or decisions affecting themselves or key people around them, or if no-one seems interested in offering an opportunity for them to state their reactions to the changes, events or decisions.

What sort of things should be explained to children?

Children should know about:

- events
- feelings
- changes
- decisions
- facts

Events

- **Before**: *what* is going to happen (i.e., preparation for an event). Even babies can be told that they are about to be taken out shopping, to go up to the bath, to go to collect their brothers and sisters from school. Even if they do not understand, your voice will be reassuring. You can even sing a little tune for each separate event so they can know what is about to happen without needing to understand language.
- **During**: *why* something is happening.
- **After**: *why* something happened (i.e., after the event, if it was unexpected).

Feelings

- how *you* are feeling
- how you imagine *they* are feeling

Changes

- absences
- routines
- partners/friends

Decisions

- Explain the reason for your decision. Do not give too many reasons because they may then appear as persuasion.

Facts

- If children ask for information about something, you should answer, or try to find out the answer if you do not already know it. 'Stop asking all those questions!' is not the right reaction.
- Less comfortable facts of life such as death or divorce should be dealt with honestly in terms which the particular child can most comfortably comprehend.

Should we explain everything? Age-appropriateness

If a child asks for an explanation about something, however difficult it might be he should be told something which at least approximates to the truth. You do not have to give long or full explanations. But distorting the truth should be avoided. There are some very good children's books telling stories which involve some sensitive issues such as going to hospital, dying, divorce or moving. Anyone who feels uncomfortable talking directly to their child about these things can always go to a local library and ask to borrow the relevant books. The issue can be raised through reading the story. It may take time and effort to make the journey, but it will be time well invested because children, like adults, hate to be kept in the dark.

Explanation and you

- If it is not obvious why something happened – why you had a row with someone, for example, or why you did not feel like doing something when someone asked you to – try asking yourself why. Looking at various explanations will help you to get closer to your own feelings and moods. Doing this will, in turn, help you to get closer to the feelings of others around you, including your child.
- Ask another person involved why something happened. If you are genuinely puzzled by another person's behaviour or reaction, get used to asking them why. There might be a simple explanation. Once you realise the good feeling you get when you know and understand things that are happening to you, you will be in a better position to see how much better your child will feel when he is forewarned or is able to understand.
- Be cautious about asking a child why he did something. (See 'Questions as power', page 71.)

EXAMPLE

From the moment of birth children learn from us. From our responses to them they learn what it is that they do which pleases us – their smiles, for example. They also copy our behaviour directly, both because they want to be like those whom they love and because they cannot help it. It happens without us being aware of it. They copy gestures and opinions, and absorb values and attitudes. Children learn, good or bad, more from us than from anywhere else, even school or television. As they get older and they are able to judge and evaluate for themselves, the influence of the parents diminishes. There are many different reasons for this. But the influence will remain potent, none the less.

Parents set an example in many aspects of life and living, some more important than others. For example, children will watch parents and any other carers and observe:

- how they treat people;
- how they spend their time;
- their attitudes to a whole range of things;
- their view of what is right and wrong;
- how they handle frustration;
- how they solve problems.

'Do as I say, not as I do!'

It is an unpleasant truth that children pay little attention when we ask them to do something that we are not willing to do ourselves. And why should they?

- Why should they stop hitting their siblings if you hit them as a punishment for doing it?
- Why should they not be allowed to shout at you if you do it to them?
- Why should they not watch television as their main leisure activity if that is how you spend much of your free time?
- If you snack throughout the day, how can you expect them to stick to eating only at meal times?
- If you are bad-tempered much of the time, how can you ask for or expect others around you to be controlled and respectful?
- If you do not put yourself out to help them or others, why should they feel like helping you?

Whatever it is that we want them to do or to

achieve, we have to make sure we apply the same standards to ourselves. This is very difficult. We may try to excuse ourselves and admit that we made a mistake in doing something, and that we do not want them to make the same mistake, or go through the same learning curve. But it will not sound very convincing. They might reply, with some justification, that they wish to be left to make their own mistakes.

If we want our children to do certain things, most of us go about achieving this through nagging and criticism. But nagging and criticism sow doubt and resentment. It is far more effective to live by our words and behave as we want them to. We need to be the model instead of the critic.

Example and you

- If we want children to do things which we find difficult, how can we begin to set a better example? We can try the 'contract approach'. This involves accepting and defining where both parties' performance falls short and setting targets for *both* sides to improve. The honesty and the shared effort will bring parties closer together, often with laughs in the process. The alternative, nagging option, by contrast, opens up chasms.

Praise; Peace; Play

PRAISE

It is good practice to:

- find one thing to praise every day
- praise the deed rather than the person
- praise the process rather than the product

Most people respond better to praise than to criticism. Yet despite knowing this, far too many of us find it easier to find fault and to judge than to give support and approval. Part of the problem is that we are out of the habit of giving praise. There is also a tendency to think that praise and approval will make our children big-headed. But the reality would seem to go deeper than either of these partial explanations. Criticism is a negative judgement. It puts the person doing the judging in a superior and slightly distant position, which gives the impression of authority. Praising someone, on the other hand, implies a sense of equality and involves giving, and therefore getting close. It is a far more uncomfortable thing to do.

What do we mean by 'praise'?

Praise can take different forms, and mean slightly different things. The dictionary defines praise as: 'Express warm approbation of; commend the merits of'. 'Praise' therefore, can mean both 'approval' and 'appreciation'.

What is the difference between the two words, and is it important?

Approve is defined as: 'confirm, accept, commend'.
Appreciate is defined as: 'estimate worth, quality, amount of; be sensitive to; esteem highly'.

In other words, 'approval' implies the whole-hearted acceptance – of the person, or of something which that person has done, without considering or evaluating in any detail why we accept that person or their product. 'Appreciation' is about worth, and valuing different qualities, especially effort. The difference between 'approval' and 'appreciation' is important. Children need to feel approved of for who they are, and appreciated for their efforts and skills.

What can we praise?

We can praise:

- choices
- ideas

- effort
- helpfulness
- independence
- thoughtfulness
- skills

The language of praise: *descriptive* praise

- Praise the deed rather than the person.

It is very easy, and very common, to use the word 'good', in relation to children. It is short, convenient, but what does it mean?

Instead of 'good', you can say 'clever', 'thoughtful', 'thanks for doing that', 'sensible', 'helpful when I needed help'.

Approval words

- That's lovely!
- That's great!
- Well done!
- Brilliant!

Appreciation words

- Thank you for doing . . .
- That was a great help to me.
- You took a lot of time and care over that.

For example, you could say:

Clothes 'That was a good choice of clothes to put on today, given the weather,' or 'Those things go nicely together' (instead of 'What a good boy to get yourself dressed!')

Ideas 'It was clever to think of doing it that way' or 'What a great idea for a game' (instead of 'You are good to have gone off and played');

Effort 'You really tried hard'; 'You did well to get so far/to do so much'; 'That model must have taken you a long time'; (instead of 'That's a good model')

Helpfulness 'Thanks for tidying away your toys'; 'It

was great that you got yourself ready for bed tonight as I am very tired'; 'Getting tea ready with me was a great help. Thanks' (instead of 'You are so good');

Independence 'You can do things very well on your own now'; 'I knew that you'd be able to do that'; 'You tried so hard to do up those buttons. You must feel really proud you cracked it' (instead of 'Good boy to do up your buttons');

Thoughtfulness 'I saw you help that little boy with his shoes in the park. That was kind' (instead of 'I saw your good deed');

Skills 'That was brilliant how you did that! You're so clever at that sort of thing'; 'You can kick a ball a long way now'; 'You played well with Gemma given you'd never met her before. You're good at making friends' (instead of 'You're a good footballer').

Children's art and crafts

If your child goes to a playgroup or nursery, the chances are that she will come home every week with armfuls of paintings, drawings and, beloved most by the collecting adults, still sticky and decidedly fragile junk models. These creations are very important (see 'Play', page 107). How should you respond to these labours of love? What should you actually say? Do you lie through your teeth and declare them all to be worthy of hanging in a gallery? Should you be honest and say what you really feel about them? Should you try and identify what they are? Should you keep *all* of them, or 'bin' them as soon as her back is turned? And should you offer any advice on how to make a tree look more like a tree, or point out that, in fact, there is a neck between people's heads and bodies? If they are the only ones not coming home with dripping paintings or sticky models, does it matter?

'Are *you* pleased with it?'

Whatever it is she has done, especially if it is something that she is asking you to comment on, one way to respond is to turn it back to her and ask her what *she* thinks. Ultimately, children have to do things for their own satisfaction or to meet their own objectives, and not because it pleases us. Of course, they will want us to be pleased by their efforts; and it is more important to comment on the effort than on what they have produced. But if you say some thing is 'good', and your child does not agree, she will see your praise as false. Your approval will not help her. If, on the other hand, she is already pleased with it, you need to let her know that that is enough – that your opinion is not as important as her own. Gradually, and increasingly, she will thus learn to value and trust her own judgements and attitudes.

Is all praise good? No!

When parents do praise children, or declare their love for them, sometimes without realising it they can say things which do not, in fact, make the child feel good about herself or about what she has done. Although it is true that we do not, generally, praise enough, we need to be aware that praise is not always either *well meant* or *well received*.

Praise which is not always well-meant: manipulative praise and emotional blackmail

Saying *'I love you'* can be another way of praising, or showing approval. But it is sometimes said by parents in order to get something in return, to make the child feel guilty if she does not want to do something being asked of her. *'But I love you. Surely you will do this little thing for me!'* It can then be turned round to become *'If you really loved me, you would not think of doing what you are about to do.'*

Praise which is not always well-received: unqualified, false, and over-frequent praise

Unqualified praise: why 'good' is bad! The following conversation between a mother and her two-year-old illustrates one of the problems with unqualified praise.

Mother: I adore you!
Child: Don't adore me, Mummy.
Mother: Why not?
Child: Because I cry too much.

This brief exchange shows how difficult it can be for children to receive unqualified and generalised praise. While we all thrive on praise and appreciation, we receive it comfortably, and it really only rewards us, not only if we feel it is justified but also if we can comfortably keep up that standard. What the little girl in this incident is saying is: 'I cannot have the responsibility of always behaving in the way which pleases you and justifies your love. I am not that good. I cry a lot (which you let me know you do not like).' If you say to a child instead that you appreciate what she has done, and make it specific to an act or event, or that you love her despite or because of her faults, there is no expectation or responsibility for her to carry on pleasing, delivering, and being perfect. No-one *is* perfect. And in any case, perfection is a treadmill.

Children feel many mixed and very strong emotions about people in their family. Adults, who limit freedom and sometimes fail to deliver love when it is needed, stir up plenty of angry feelings. Brothers and sisters are also frequently objects of hatred as they are rivals for attention and approval. Children's fantasy is highly volatile and imaginative. There will be many moments of intense hatred, fear, loathing and resentment when they can wish the worst on those around them. To be told, close to one of these moments of private intrigue and wickedness, that they are 'good' can cause not only guilt and confusion, but also a sense of failure at not being able to live up to expectations. They will also feel a need to hide the wicked bits of themselves. It will be far better to say, *'I bet you wished you could kick your brother then. Well done for only thinking it'* than *'Weren't you good not to hurt your brother today.'*

False praise Children will see through praise which is patently false. They will be as sensitive to insincerity as we are. However, we all like a little flattery. There is a significant difference between unnecessary praise and false praise. The word 'flattery' is used to cover both forms. Unnecessary praise may be used to get on the good side of someone, but at least it is the truth. False praise is offensive.

Over-frequent praise Too much praise diminishes its value.

Praise and presents

Praise is showing appreciation in words. Presents are another way of saying thank you and expressing love. It is a joy to see the surprised delight in a child's eyes when they receive something unexpected. Giving gives us pleasure, too. But presents should not become a substitute for words. Children value both ways of showing love.

Praise and conceit

Many people feel uncomfortable with the idea of praising their children. For them, it smacks of flattery. We grow up believing that it is better to slap children down, to put them in their place, than to encourage them to have pride in their achievements – in case this encourages conceit.

When a child believes that his particular abilities makes him *better as a person* than others without those talents, and when that belief causes him to *look down on others* and consider them inferior, the child does, indeed, come across as an unpleasant prig. But this undue *conceit* does not have to follow from having a legitimate pride and confidence in the things which he can do well. As long as 'good at' is not seen to be the same thing as 'better than' in anything other than comparative skill terms, it is important to let children know when and at what they have done well.

To guard against inappropriate conceit, you can again apply the distinction between the **deed** and the **person**. You can be impressed by what your child can do; but it should not make you value him as an individual any more or less. As soon as you begin to confuse the two, you enter dangerous territory. If he begins to brag about his achievements, it might be because this is the only means by which he can value himself.

You should be able to encourage a legitimate pride without this developing into conceit if you:

- **value your child** for *who he is*, and **praise him** for *what he has done*;
- ensure that you **value a variety of skills** so that your child learns tolerance;
- teach that '**good at**' means '**different from**', not *'better than'*.

Praise is undoubtedly important to a child's sense of value and worth. But be careful how you give it. Remember: you are generally on safe ground if you:

- appreciate rather than approve;
- praise the deed rather than the person;
- praise the process rather than the product.

Praise and you

- Ask for it if you want to hear it.
- Tell yourself, and believe it, if you think you did something well.
- Reward yourself.
- The more you show you appreciate others, the more likely they are to show that they appreciate you.
- If someone praises you, accept it and hold on to it. Don't squirm or hand it back, saying you don't deserve it, or 'it was nothing'. Just say 'Thank you.'

PEACE

Children, just as much as anyone else, need time and space to relax and wind down, a time to feel at rest and at ease with themselves. Everyone has their own way of unwinding. Some people need to flop in front of the television for a while. Some need to be alone, to 'fiddle about' aimlessly – with their toys, or in the garden. Some like to kick a ball, or bury themselves in the newspaper, or soak in a bath. Others like to sit with a cup of tea, or have a beer at the bar. Whatever it is, we all need it. We don't always get it, or take it. But which particular thing we choose to do to unwind says something important about who we are. Being quiet during these times gives us a chance to let our thoughts roam. It is a time to reflect and, most important, to find out what is inside us and to learn to be happy with ourselves.

Peace means:

- the chance to wind down and relax, or even escape
- calm
- quiet togetherness
- being alone
- rest
- sleep

- silence
- the absence of arguments and tension

We do not have to be alone to experience this regenerating peace. We can be quiet with others there, too. We need opportunities to realise that relationships can exist without words, that we can still feel togetherness without action and conversation; in other words, that silence as communion can be a form of communication and that someone's company is enough to make you feel at ease. One of the limitations of the 'quality time' which some working parents try to give their children when they get home is that it tends to be action-packed. There will be a lot of talk. There may be games. The child may be asked to describe her day when her mind has wandered a long way away from earlier events. The time given to the child is too contrived. It pays no attention to her mood and does not acknowledge the value of quiet togetherness and spontaneity. There is too much 'ought' about the socialising, with the child being 'booked in' to the parents' day, and not enough 'want'.

If the atmosphere at home is so emotionally charged and difficult – or just busy and crowded – that it cannot readily offer restful space, perhaps a relative, friend or neighbour could provide the bolt hole instead.

Action plan

- Discover their mechanisms for winding down.
- Encourage them to do it.
- Respect their need for their own space, even if it is not in your home.
- Encourage quiet togetherness – e.g., watch TV together, give time for morning cuddles in bed if they are young enough, or sit with them silently stroking their face as they go to sleep.

Peace and you

You need to give yourself peaceful time:

- to reflect;
- to regain the strength to cope;
- to reassure yourself that you can be content with your own company – that you can be your own friend.

If you need to be busy all the time, ask yourself why, and make yourself sit, quietly and alone, and see how it makes you feel and what you get from it.

Your action plan

- Identify your own mechanisms for winding down.
- Try to spend fifteen minutes every day 'with your feet up', at rest, however you like to do it.
- Try to have some quiet togetherness with those who are close to you.

PLAY

Through play, children:

- find out who they are
- discover what they can do
- realise they can manage on their own

Finding out who they are: developing self-esteem

It would be hard to over-emphasise the importance of play in children's development and, in particular, the development of their self-esteem. Play is, and should be, about choices. As children play, they make many choices. They have to choose *what* to play. They have to choose *where* to play. They may be able to choose *who to play with*. If they are painting or colouring, they have to choose what to draw, and *which colour* to do it in. If they are playing imaginatively, with others or by themselves, they have to choose *the story-line*, which *characters* are to be in the story and, most importantly, who *they* are going to be. If they are playing ball with friends, they have to choose *the rules* which will apply. If they are dressing up, they have to choose *what to put on*. All of these choices help to build up a picture of themselves – what they like to do, who they like to be with – and gives them a sense of being in control of their lives. Making choices in the context of play makes the experience of choosing easy and 'safe'. They are safe because there is no right or wrong decision. 'Make believe', cutting paper, arranging bricks or squishing modelling material can take any form. Nothing hangs on it. Identity and confidence can develop, unrestrained by fear of mistake and failure. As children get older, and their identity is better established, they are more able to cope with the challenge of play which is structured and governed by rules – which has winners and losers. Play with few or no choices, on the other hand – the kind of play which is tightly managed by an adult – can teach certain things. But what it does not provide is opportunities to reveal, without fear or failure, what it is which makes you 'you'.

Discovering what they can do: developing self-confidence

Play develops many skills – physical, social and intellectual. Imaginative play helps to develop language (because children chatter as they invent) and the ability to create stories. It also helps with social skills, teaching how to approach and get on with others, compromise or negotiate. Running and climbing develops physical co-ordination. Being in control of their own bodies, and being strong and vigorous, is often children's first experience of real pride and achievement. Physical activity also promotes a general fitness which will not only have life-long benefits but will also contribute to stamina and competence in a wide range of tasks. Play helps children to develop problem-solving skills and planning skills. Experiencing failures outside the real world where it does not matter helps them to manage and cope with failure when they do have to account for it. Playing with others introduces children to different ideas, hobbies and ways of thinking which enriches their experience and gives them a wider range of resources on which to draw.

Realising they can manage on their own: developing self-reliance

Children need opportunities to play and experiment free from adult supervision and scrutiny; and they need this more the older they get. If we hover over them, ready to solve any little problem which arises, they cannot learn to cope on their own. As children get older they need – in the safety of a group – to venture further afield and explore the world outside their home. It may be comfortable for us to have our children safely indoors watching TV, or travelling somewhere with us; but such protection may not be in their long-term best interests.

Sharing their play

While children need the chance to explore their experiences and feelings, alone and separate from the adult's critical eye, there are times when a child needs you to join in, provided that you don't then take it over. Your child's play may seem daft, and you will almost certainly feel daft. But you are needed not only to provide the role which he is examining but also so that he may validate himself because you *accept* his play which is *his* creation. It is essential that parents give children opportunities for spontaneous play, particularly for imaginative play, and show an interest in what their children play. Children's play must never be belittled, or their fantasy shattered. When you play with your child, he will believe that you play the game with him because you enjoy and love him so much. How can you make sure that you do not direct and interfere with his play?

Don't undermine your child by capping or improving his ideas. Adult ideas will invariably be more sophisticated than a child's. By improving your child's ideas you don't teach him how to do it better next time – only that his ideas and he himself fall short and are not good enough. If you want to suggest options to extend his thinking, keep them for next time and offer them before the play starts.

Don't devalue aimless play. Again, the shape it eventually takes (and it almost certainly will take on a shape) is a measure of the child's creative abilities and his growing sense of identity – who he is and what he likes and does not like. Force him to do something which *you* recognise as purposeful and you are not only in danger of imposing your view of what is 'appropriate' play, but also transmitting that you do not trust his choice or approve of what he does to 'be himself'. This could be interpreted as not approving of who he is.

Some children find it difficult to play. They need some help to have and be confident about ideas, and they need to learn how to be creative and develop story-lines. If you have a child who seems to freeze up when asked to 'play something', perhaps you could play with him and carefully guide him through a range of possibilities. This may be difficult for you. Many adults feel desperately uncomfortable with childlike fantasy. But children are not necessarily aware of this discomfort. You could start by involving them in the normal, daily things that you do and then acting these out with their cuddly toys. Sitting down with paper and crayons and drawing together is another easy way into the child's world.

Imaginative play

Imaginative play is a child's opportunity for the most individualised creativity totally free from the frustrations and constrictions of undeveloped skills. It frees the mind. Fantasy allows endless possibilities. Play, therefore, also develops mental agility and flexibility. In imaginative play, there are no ground rules which have been set by anyone else either of a structured, game-oriented type or of a physical nature (for example, hold the pencil this way, don't mess up the colours in the paintbox, don't let it drop on the floor). If the activity exists in the child's imagination, nothing can go wrong. They are in a world beyond criticism and beyond practical mishap where they are not only **safe** but also in **control**. If you join in with them, they not only control the fantasy but it also enables them, in a sense, to control you. We are back again to the all-important dimension of power in the adult-child relationship. Children do feel acutely their lack of power compared with adults. If they feel that power is abused, they will try and get their own back by developing all sorts of manipulative strategies. Give them plenty of chances to be on the other side of the fence and wield the power in play and fantasy, as well as in real choices about their life, and the need to manipulate and get their own back – to play power back at you – will diminish.

Play as therapy

Entering children's play and giving them the opportunity to control you either by active role reversal or just by letting them control the events of the fantasy/drama, may well release resentment. It should not now need to be said that, when you enter that fantasy, you must not start to direct it. Play along with it, yes. Shape it and develop the events in your allocated role, yes. There is a big difference between the statement *'Let's do it this way'* and *'How do you think it would work if we did it this way?'* But if you take it over, or if you undermine it by transferring in and out of the makebelieve to your real world to do forgotten jobs, thereby indicating that you don't take it seriously and respect their needs, the time you have spent with them may well have been wasted.

Play also gives children a chance to act out situations which they soon have to face, which they are currently going through, or which they have recently been through in order to sort things out – to become more familiar and comfortable with changes and perhaps to increase their understanding, and thereby their sense of security. They may want, and need, to play the same things over and over again. The same benefit can be gained from reading stories about events which can be stressful. When children are going into hospital or starting school for the first time, they will often become almost obsessed with books describing what is likely to happen, or telling a story around the life change, wanting to have them read to them repeatedly. At times of change and stress, children should have relevant books or play materials close by to look at and exploit if they feel the need.

Play is also a useful tool for parents to use

to relieve both their own and their child's anxiety by replaying something that happened. It seems to be particularly useful to the child for the parent or carer to change places with them – with the adult being the naughty child, for example, making the incident quite ridiculous and turning it into the safe arena of farce. Humour can heal a great deal. For example, if you play a 'let's pretend' game about going out shopping, you can include fights over buying sweets, arguments over how many packets of biscuits you will get, and sulks about having to go out in the first place. Role reversal can also be used effectively when you think your child feels resentful about being overpowered. Another technique is to use dolls or soft toys to take on different characters, to replay something which happened in the family or at school – being told off, for example.

All changes are stressful, particularly those which overturn established routines. This is as true for children as it is for us. We can talk through any anxieties which we have with our friends, but young children cannot. We can explore our own relationships and difficulties through reading novels or going to the cinema. Young children cannot. Play is the only route for them to work through their insecurities and to explore the possibilities. Art and music, the other expressive outlets, may help to release tensions, anger or other emotions, **but they cannot be as effective as play in working out solutions and strategies for the problems which children encounter in their world.**

Play and television

Watching television is a form of leisure, but it is not play. It can provide ideas to be used in play (craft ideas or scenarios for 'let's pretend') and it can be used to wind down and relax, but it would be a mistake to say that television is, or offers the same kind of experience as, quality play.

Leisure is normally understood as free time, time at your own disposal to do what you like with. **Play**, according to the dictionary, is 'moving about in a lively manner', 'amusing oneself', 'pretending for fun', or 'being involved in a game'. Broadcast television, as distinct from video games displayed on a television screen, does not qualify under any of these definitions.

If choices are an important part of **quality play** (that is, play which enhances the self and offers scope for experiment and personal development), television certainly cannot qualify. What choices, apart from changing the channel, or pressing the on/off button, does it offer? Television can inform; television can educate; television can offer a variety of models of relationships for children to observe. Sitcoms or drama on television can extend children's concepts of experience and fiction, and give them insights into relationships and situations which might be troubling them personally. **But television cannot build on or manifest a child's inner resources for coping, develop her powers of intuition, or deepen her sense of herself, as profoundly as does the 'hands-on' experience of play.**

Quality play involves:

- choices
- imagination
- other people, real or created
- experiment

So: **make space** for them to play in; **make time** to play with them; and make sure that some of this time is spent in **makebelieve**.

What can they play?

Unstructured or 'free' play

Creative play is pre-social play which children can do on their own before they are able to play co-operatively or sustain complex story-lines. (For example, painting, using soft modelling materials, drawing, cutting and sticking.) Creative play develops manipulative skills, ideas, encourages experimentation, develops confidence in making choices, and offers a channel for children to explore themselves and their talents.

Imaginative play encourages inventiveness, putting ideas into words, inter-personal and problem-solving skills.

Physical play develops strength and co-ordination, both of which are needed for early experiences of competence.

Structured play: rule-governed and 'directional'

Rule-governed play (for example, team sports or board or card games) develops notions of 'fairness' and co-operation in all players if everyone abides by the rules.

'Directional' play is non-competitive (for example, jigsaws and craft skills). It encourages 'stickability', or task commitment – the ability to stay with a task or activity until it is completed.

Play and you

Play and enjoy yourself so you feel happy and fulfilled and not resentful. If you enjoy doing a number of different things, your child will learn:

- how to use time constructively;
- that you like to play;
- that you have needs, too, which are part of your boundaries and which have to be respected.

Trust; Touch; Time; Talk

TRUST

A fundamental and mutual trust is created between mother and infant at birth. It is almost imprinted, since the notion of trust implies an expectation and can therefore only really develop after some experiences over time (however short) which establish that expectation. At the moment of birth, however, the infant must trust that the mother will care and provide for her, and the mother trusts, on her part, that the infant will love and need her. If the mother does not believe that that will be the case, then why should she bother to take on the responsibility of rearing the child? It is the infinite, or at least undefined, degree of need for care and nurture which both triggers the instinct to care and love in the mother (in most instances) yet also can terrify her so much that she withdraws into a depression in order to hold on to her self.

So, from the very beginning, an unspoken and reciprocated simple trust exists. As he grows older, if you do not trust your child, it amounts to the same thing as putting him down. Growing up involves facing new things – situations and experiences – at a rate which most adults would find enormously stressful. It takes great courage to embark on something new. You really have to believe in yourself to cope with new things confidently. Imagine the hurt, and the body blow to your pride, if the person you rely on most for your evaluation of yourself assumes that you are unlikely to be able to achieve a particular thing – often before you have even really tried.

Trust your child

- Trust your child's **competence** – his ability to achieve something. *'Shall I help you?'* while seeming supportive, in fact sends a message that you don't think he is going to manage the task at hand.

- Trust his **ability to complete something**. Always put the past behind. Let him start each new venture or attempt with a clean sheet of expectations.
- Trust his **judgement**.
- Trust his sense of **responsibility**.
- Trust, and praise, his **ideas**.

Don't abuse your child's trust in you

Trust and you

- Trust your ability to be a 'positive parent'.
- Trust that your child needs and wants you more than he wants anyone else.
- Trust the relationship you have with your child, which will have its natural ups and downs. Try not to test out his love, curry favour, or to interpret his disappointments as a rejection of you. Parents have to be parents first, and friends second.

*T*OUCH

Never withdraw your body; give your child somewhere safe to hide

For some reason, we in Western societies seem to have lost the habit of touching each other. We are very happy to spend hours fondling our pets and really enjoy the pleasure they seem to get from it. We enjoy it too, relishing their soft fur. Indeed, stroking them has a physical, calming effect on us with such a powerful effect on our biological functions that animals are now used therapeutically to help people recover from surgery and stress-related illnesses. Despite this, we seem to be totally insensitive to the need of our fellow human beings, adults and children, for the warmth, reassurance and pure physical pleasure which comes from touching, stroking and caressing. This is in contrast to Eastern cultures where the therapeutic value of touch and massage has been acknowledged for centuries. It is certainly not considered appropriate for mature adults, outside a growing romantic relationship, to walk about with their arms round each other or hold hands. It is even becoming less common for people to touch by the more formal method of shaking hands. Why?

Quite simply, we are getting out of the habit of touching, and to touch 'feels' like an increasingly strange and difficult thing to do. But there may be more to it than that. Touching is also an important expression of giving, and a sign of equality and empathy (hence the contrived political handshake and arm squeeze); and fewer people today seem to be able to give – to feel equal and sufficiently confident to make that physical statement of giving.

A child who is not touched is a child who will feel ignored, ashamed, unworthy of attention, inferior and misunderstood. In short, that child will feel lost, alone, unsure and unhappy.

We touch our new babies, of course, when they are fed and have their nappies changed. But the mother who does more, and ties her baby to her front or props her on her hip while she walks about and does other things, is generally told off and accused of spoiling the child. When we no longer feed our children and they manage their own toileting, somehow the touching often disappears too. It is very important for *all* adults involved in caring to touch. Maternal touch is assumed to be more important than the male or paternal touch. But fathers, stepfathers, and live-in boyfriends all need to think about the child's need to be accepted and approved by them. Of course, we need to be aware of the important cultural, gender and legal differences between appropriate and inappropriate touching. This appeal to recognise a child's need for physical affection should not be interpreted as an invitation to engage in inappropriate or abusive behaviour. But anyone who has a sufficiently close and regular relationship with a child such that the child begins to assess and understand herself through that relationship, must acknowledge the child's need to know that they are loved and believed in as can be expressed so spontaneously through appropriate touch.

Touch has a language of its own. It can say so much, in so many different ways, and it need take only a split second. It can be a full embrace. It can be an arm around the shoulders. It can ask for nothing in return, or it can demand something back, an equal response or at least an acknowledgement that the hidden message has been received.

It is a mistake just to touch children when *you* need it; when you need reassurance, to feel loved, or to calm down after a stressful experience. Touching them only at these times comes close to treating children like pets. Of course, children can give us enormous consolation when we are upset. Their love replenishes us when we are down. But what about when *they* are down? What about *their* need for reassurance and consolation? If they come to us for a cuddle when *they* feel they need it, do we accept it even if it is not desperately convenient? Or do we put the thing we are busy with first? It can be very damaging to their pride, and therefore dangerous to your relationship, to reject spontaneous expressions of affection. Beneath the behaviour, good or bad, that they are showing you, there will be not only very complex emotions but also a desperate need to love you and to be loved by you. The touch they want to give you is saying something which they could not possibly put into words. It will say: 'I need you. I am sorry. Please tell me, by accepting my touch, that you still want *me* even though my behaviour has been awful.' It would be even better if we could get in first, reading the signs in advance that what they really need is understanding and reassurance.

Touch is:

- intimate
- a statement of human equality
- a quicker form of expression than words
- less liable to misinterpretation
- an important gesture of giving
- implies mutual understanding

Kinds of touching

- **One-way**: giving.
- **Two-way**: giving and receiving.
- **The habitual or ritual touch** (for example, first thing in the morning, after school, returning from a friend) may seem superficial, but it is advisable to keep the practice of touching in the family so that in the difficult times, when showing affection is hard, it is easier to maintain it.)
- **The spontaneous touch** really means something particular to the individual child – an expression of understanding of a particular experience they are having.

The vocabulary of touch

The accepting touch

- the possessive (in the best sense) touch: *'You belong to me'*
- the healing touch – after the argument

- the understanding/consoling touch
- the proud touch
- the equality touch: *'I am the same/feel the same as you'*
- the loving touch

The rejecting touch

Touch is so powerful that it is also used negatively to reject and to hurt – not to cause pain, which it can obviously do, but to hurt feelings.

- the push away (how do *you* feel when your cuddle is pushed away? Doesn't it speak volumes?)
- the quick slap

When your cuddle/touch is brushed away: the 'snail' effect When a cuddle is rejected, what does it mean? It does not mean that your child hates you for ever. It is most likely to happen after an argument, and it means that the child has been hurt. Like a snail whose antennae are poked, a child will recoil and be wary of accepting the cuddle in case the renewed trust is mistaken and the poking starts again. It is essential that you do not, then, recoil yourself. Instead, you should acknowledge the feelings. Don't force the cuddle, but say that you are there and ready to receive her physical approach when she feels ready to give it.

Touch and you

What can you do if you are still finding it difficult to be closer physically to your child?

- Ask your partner to massage/stroke/hug you so that you can appreciate the benefits of this contact. Often, releasing the block in one part of your life can release it in others, too.

- If you have no partner, or your partner does not want to, then ask a friend, or pay for a professional massage.
- To make it easier, think of a touching activity to do with your child which is not displaying emotion. You could try sitting next to her while watching TV, or stroking her forehead as she settles to sleep.

TIME

- Your child needs *you* and, sometimes, your complete and undivided attention.
- Don't let bad behaviour be the only way of getting attention.
- Presents are no substitute for presence.

Why is spending time with your child so important?

For children to get any sense that they are loved and wanted, you have to be prepared to spend time with them. There is no getting away from this simple truth. If you do not give them very much of your time, talking, laughing, playing, sharing things or just generally being around listening to and enjoying them, how can they possibly get any other message than that they are not worthy of your love, time and attention? How can they then progress to love themselves if they perceive that you always put yourself and others first, before them, and that they are apparently incidental to your life – even that they are a nuisance? And their need does not stop at five, when they first go to school. They go on needing you to be interested in them and to *demonstrate* your love for them by spending time with them right through adolescence.

How do we know that children need so much time?

- The more you give, the more they want.
- If they do not get it, they behave badly to try and get it.

Your child will need you, love you and want you more than you can imagine. You give him his sense of belonging, his security. His need for you can seem insatiable. The more you give, it seems, the more he wants. That can be terrifying, especially if you do not feel ready to give that much; for example, if you are still exploring yourself. When children are little, they crave time and attention so badly that, if it is not given naturally and spontaneously, they will behave in whatever outrageous way they have to in order to get it. Bad behaviour is a very effective way of getting attention. If you let it be the only way to get you to take notice of them, you are unlikely to see any change in it, however much you discipline and punish. The cycle of poor behaviour and self-doubt can very easily turn first to self-hatred, and then to full-scale opting out of the system.

Time to do what?

Talk	Talk about your day, their day, what you are going to do, what you are seeing in the street, what you have been watching on television, what they like to do, your childhood, their relatives, their toys.
Play	Sit with them while they play, and talk to them about what they are doing.
Listen	Look at their faces when they are telling you something. If it seems important, stop what you are doing and sit down with them to hear it.
Quiet time	Sit with them while they watch TV or while they get ready for bed.

Share	Invite them to do something or go somewhere with you, to show you enjoy their company: *'Come and talk to me while I get tea ready.'*

In other words, you can:

- join them in what *they* are doing;
- invite them to join you in what *you* are doing;
- do something alongside them, in parallel, talking together or just being quiet together.

Special time for each one

Each child in the family ideally needs to have their own special time with each of their parents. It does not have to take a vast amount of time, or have to happen every day. But each child is different, and will want to have a chance to be alone with each of you. At the root of sibling rivalry lies competition for the parents' attention. Clearly defined, individual, 'special' time given to each child in a family can lead to a marked reduction in the fights between them.

Special time can be:

- reading to them on their own at bedtime, though this is not always practical;
- sitting with them while they or you have a bath, or having a bath together, if they are young enough and do not mind;
- having one of them read or talk to you while you do the ironing or any DIY chores;
- walking to the bus stop with them if they are older and going out somewhere.

There are many different ways to give special time. It may need to be different with each child to match their needs and interests.

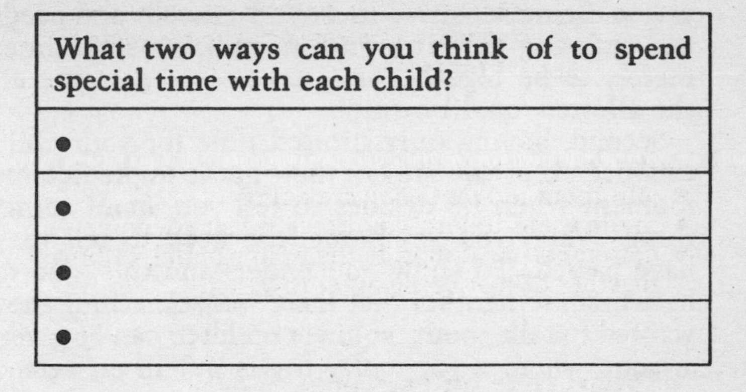

What two ways can you think of to spend special time with each child?

-
-
-
-

'Quality time'

'Quality time' is an approach which has been developed to meet the working parent's main predicament – not being able to spend very much time at home. The idea of 'quality time' suggests that it is not *how much* time we spend with our children which matters but that what is important is *what we do with them* when we are around. In other words, **quality** is seen as more important than **quantity**.

Spending 'quality time' with our children means giving them our whole-hearted attention, and ensuring it is constructive, productive time spent actively *doing* things with them. 'Quality time' is therefore often seen as action-packed time or, at least, a socially intense time. It is a very important concept but its limitations should be understood so that we can meet children's needs more effectively.

First, 'quality time' does not always take account of moods and feelings. Instead of doing something active – having to play or talk – at the appointed time, a child may feel like being quiet with you, curling up with their favourite cuddly toy. **Communion**, or quiet togetherness, can be just as important for the relationship as active **communication**. Being sensitive to a child's moods and needs and realising that it is just as valuable sometimes merely to be together may take some pressure off the allotted 'quality time'.

Second, having only limited time for your child can mean that you are not there at the unpredictable moment when he decides to tell you about something. When you get home, the need to tell may have passed. To show you understand this, and to help them remember that there was something they wanted to talk about, younger children can be given a game where a particular toy is put in an agreed place where you will see it when you come in. Older children can make a note of things they want to raise, so there can be a family message pad or noticeboard hung on a wall (or fridge) for general use.

Third, children can be told where appropriate that although time for actually doing things together may be limited, a parent can always be reached during the working day by telephone if there is a special problem.

'Being there' for children does not have to mean twenty-four-hour availability but it does mean offering some flexibility on access to meet special circumstances and listening to them when they ask for it.

Time and television

Research has shown that children who watch a lot of television have significantly lower self-esteem than those who do not. This is nothing to do with what they watch, and the effect it might have on them. The low self-esteem is explained by the fact that the time spent watching is time children are *not* spending talking to their parents. They therefore get no sense of being valued, of the adults they are close to wanting to spend time with them. So rather than just nagging them to turn off the TV, next time why not try offering to do or play something with them instead?

Time for you
- Try to make some time free for you to enjoy doing whatever it is you like to do.
- If having 'special time' alone with your partner will help you to feel wanted and valued, ask for it and organise it.

*T*ALK (and listen!)

Talking to your child will:
- **enhance** the relationship
- **engage** his attention
- **enliven** him, making him feel interesting and wanted

The importance of talking to children

Talking to children helps to develop:
- their **language skills** – their ability to express themselves and communicate;
- their sense of having a **unique relationship** with you;
- their sense of **value and self**;
- their **social competence**.

Talking to children is extremely important, for two reasons: **first**, children need language to be able to **communicate** with others It helps them express themselves and to fit in with others. They have to use words to show what they know – in school, for example. The more adults talk to children and babies, the easier children will find it to use and to understand words and the better they will manage their education. Second, talking is a way of **showing that you care**. Children who are not spoken to will feel ignored and unimportant. Talking to them, involving them, asking about what has happened to them and telling them things which have happened to you, all send the message that you think they are important. Talking, therefore, is essential to creating good self-esteem.

The importance of listening to children

Listening to children helps to develop:

- their sense of being **understood**;
- their feelings of being **acknowledged and respected**;
- their feelings of being **trusted**;
- their need to have somewhere **safe to go to be honest**;
- their need to have someone who is **there for them**.

Listening to children involves more than hearing their words. We must also 'hear' their actions. What children *do* can speak volumes about what is happening inside their heads. Words are not the only currency of communication.

Beware too much talk, and using words as tools of power and control

Adults can use words to:

- **entangle**, through using logic and reason which is too sophisticated and difficult for children to understand;
- **entrap**, tripping them up, as in a courtroom, through clever questions;
- **engulf**, smother and swamp children's feelings. When children are pre-verbal, they feel, they perceive. When words develop, they can be used to conceal.

Quality talk

'Quality talk' is talking *to* someone and opening up the conversation so that it becomes two-way, with each person **listening** to and **hearing** the other. When we talk to our children, we must make sure we say things which start a conversation, which encourage them to join in. This is very different from 'talking at' someone, when we direct comments or questions but seem disinterested in the other person's reactions. The two approaches can be illustrated thus:

Talk to → Message listened to → Answer/Respond → An opening/expanding exchange

Talk at → Message bounces off → Incident ignored → A closed-off exchange

'Talking at' will include asking children a question, and then answering it for them. For example, *'What would you like to drink? I know, milk's your favourite at the moment, so I'll get you that.'*

What can you talk about?

Anything. Babies are happy with just the sound of our voices, so when children are very small we can simply describe whatever it is we are doing. Later, we can talk about what we have done during the day, what we have read in a magazine, or what we have seen on television. We can ask about their day – what they enjoyed, who they talked to. Later still, when some of those questions may be rejected as prying, if we focus on the things which interest them we can try to keep the lines of communication open.

Talk and you

- If you want someone to talk to you, ask for it!

EmpathISE; SympathISE; ApologISE; CompromISE

EMPATH*ISE*

'My mum doesn't understand me!'

Teenagers often feel misunderstood. Although they would probably prefer to be understood by their parents, if they are not, they will not be alone in the world – most will have a sizeable group of friends who will be on the same wavelength and with whom they identify. In fact, adolescents typically group to boost their confidence and sense of identity and belonging while they come to terms with the idea of growing away from their parents.

Young children do not have that luxury. A child who feels misunderstood will also feel very much alone. She cannot consult her friends in playgroup or infant school, asking if they feel the same way. The very thought of such a discussion is ludicrous. Even if such things were discussed, most would find it well nigh impossible to put such intangible feelings and experiences into words.

Most people who live closely together, especially parents and children, develop an intuitive sense about each other. When babies are small and cannot talk, we rely totally on intuition to understand how they are feeling – why they are crying. It starts off as guesswork, but we gradually build an understanding of our child's patterns and personality. It is often easier said than done. You can feel extremely stupid taking your nearly new baby to the doctor over something which worries you and being unable to answer their question, 'Is she normally like this?' In reality, you still have not got a clue what is normal. Every day they seem to be different. Even when we do feel more in touch, we start by interpreting their cries and communications in terms of physiological needs – hunger, too hot or too cold, tummy pain – rather than emotional feelings. We tend not to consider that the helpless infant can also feel bored, isolated, frightened, angry or in desperate need of the security of a cuddle.

The normal range of physiological needs do, in fact, tell us something about individuals. We can learn that our children have their own individual body rhythms. For example, one might like to eat most at midday, while another might feel most hungry after school. One might never seem to feel the cold, while another might need to wear many layers even in summer. Of course, children have to learn to adjust and fit into a family routine. But this need not involve them losing their identity if their individual patterns are understood and acknowledged.

Apart from our basic physiological blueprint, it is our 'finer' feelings, or the lack of them, which make us who we are and which give us our sense of self. That certain things frustrate us, make us happy, interest us, upset us, or hurt us makes us who we are. We could not be 'us' if we did not feel and react in this particular way to those particular things. If, as parents, we are able to recognise these 'particularities', and to understand, therefore, not only where our children are coming from but also show some respect for how they see their world, we will be able to empathise with them. Empathy means being able to know, or to have a good guess, how they might be feeling about something and that it is real for them. You do not have to agree with their view. But if you can at least appreciate *their* dilemma, at *their* level, they will not feel the pain of isolation or the puzzlement and grief of losing your support. We can only empathise with someone if we have some personal experience of our own which lets us know what it means to, for example, lose a pet (bereavement) or come last in a race (failure and humiliation). Either we have had similar experiences or we have had feelings close enough to allow us to enter imaginatively into someone else's feelings. Someone who has never experienced such feelings or who is completely out of touch with their own feelings, cannot empathise, they can only sympathise.

Understanding a child should not be especially difficult. It rarely involves more than understanding ourselves and acknowledging feelings from the past. However, this can be tricky. Many of us bury our own feelings so deep that it is hard or painful to get back in touch with them. But it will enrich our lives if we can go back. Getting close to our children can be a doubly rewarding experience if we can also get back in touch with ourselves – even if it does mean reflecting on some uncomfortable things. You will need to:

- **talk** to your child;
- **listen** to what she says about her feelings;
- **hear** what her actions say about her wishes, pleasures and pains;
- **be open and honest** with yourself and with her; this will help to release your feelings.

Openness and honesty go hand in hand with empathy.

What does empathy mean in practice?

'When my ten-year-old son left his swimming things at home on swimming day for the second week running, and the third time that term, I was as mad as anything. But I knew that he hadn't done it on purpose. I realised that there was no point in giving him a hard time, because it would make no difference to whether he would forget them another week. I realised how awful it must have been for

him, sitting out again and feeling so stupid. When he got home I said, 'It must have been so awful for you, feeling so embarrassed and stupid in front of the teacher and the whole class.' 'You're right', he replied. He never forgot them again.'

We often throw out questions which imply that we are accusing our children of something, such as:

- *'Why do you insist on wearing those ludicrous clothes?'*
- *'Why do you spend all day in front of the television?'*
- *'Why do you always hit your sister?'*
- *'Why must you always get so dirty?'*
- *'Why are you such a fidget?'*

Instead, we can try seeing it from their point of view. We can guess at their answer, and voice it for them, showing that we are attempting to understand them. We can then rephrase our questions so they become more like statements:

- *'That outfit is obviously a favourite. Is that what everyone's wearing now? Can't say I go for it!'*
- *'I think you must be feeling bored.'*
- *'I realise that you sometimes feel angry at your sister, but hitting her isn't the way to show it.'*
- *'You get so carried away with your games, you don't think of my pile of washing, do you?'*
- *'It seems hard for you to sit still at the table for the whole meal. I used to feel wriggly, too.'*

Empathy is practical

A parent who can show that she understands what her child is feeling will be more successful at getting him to do things he does not, initially, want to. He will not feel put down or put upon. He will not feel ignored. He will not feel resentful. Empathy is the best way to demonstrate to your child not only that you can be on the same wavelength as him, but also that you are still there for him . . . **and that you are on his side**.

Empathy and you

- Ask your children and your partner to see things from your point of view. Either ask them to listen, and tell them what it is, or invite them to imagine what your *reasons* might be.
- Invite them also to consider how you might *feel* about something which has happened or which they have done.

SYMPATH*ISE*

To sympathise means to share what someone is feeling. Sympathy is different from empathy. While empathy with a child involves *understanding* and getting close to what an experience means for them, sympathy just requires us to exercise compassion and commiseration that tells them it is OK to be feeling the way they do – their feelings are legitimate.

Sometimes we fail to give sympathy because we hate our children to be sad, disappointed or hurt. We want to pretend that they are really all right and we press them to feel better. If we have been responsible for their disappointment, we may feel guilty, so there is even more reason to want them to 'get over it' quickly. The assumption is that if we ask or tell them to stop feeling, this will influence the matter. It won't. Whatever reasons we may offer to help disperse the feelings, they won't want to hear them. They only feel their disappointment, sadness or pain and are aware that we seem not to appreciate the scale of what they feel. If we do not at least accept their feelings, and say something like, *'That's a big hurt, isn't it?'* the message children receive will be *'my mother expects me to be more reasonable and mature than I can be.'*

APOLOG*ISE*

An apology is a sign of strength, not weakness

Many people believe that if they apologise to a child, they weaken themselves and the rules they are trying to keep. They also believe it will make the child think their behaviour was OK after all. It is important to realise that this need not be so.

You can apologise for what *you* did, how you responded to a child's behaviour, without condoning or accepting what *the child* did. This distinction can be important.

Apologising in this way makes it clear that you are not weakening the rules. It will not be a sign of weakness. It will not be the start of a behavioural slippery slope down towards chaos. It will not undermine your authority – your ability to make the rules or to expect compliance. It *will* set a good example and encourage your child to be open and apologise when he has done wrong.

Apologising demonstrates:

- **equality** in terms of human rights
- **empathy** for what you might have done to their feelings
- **respect** for their right to be treated fairly

Apologising is similar to praise. If you are feeling vulnerable and playing power, and trying to keep a position of safe distance and superiority, it is something you do not do. If, on the other hand, you feel strong and not threatened, you will not feel you lose anything important by doing it.

Apologising teaches that:

- you can admit error without loss of face
- your self-esteem is strong enough to be left intact
- you are prepared to take responsibility
- everyone makes mistakes sometimes
- you, and your child, can survive mistakes

Admitting error and taking responsibility

Apologising involves taking responsibility for your behaviour and accepting that you did something wrong which you regret. It also means that *you* take responsibility (and at the same take it *away from* the child) for the sequence of events linked to your regretted reaction – which is frequently part of a downward spiral of increasingly unpleasant and unseemly behaviour which the child will be feeling very uncomfortable about.

If you do not formally accept responsibility for your behaviour, and yet you none the less feel bad about what you did or what has happened, you might feel tempted to dump your bad feelings on someone else. You might make someone else responsible for it by **laying the blame** elsewhere. People frequently blame others near by for things which are either nobody's fault, or are really their own fault. When you are passing the responsibility over to children, and blaming them, this is usually extremely unfair. You will make them feel guilty and **resentful**.

If you find that you frequently blame others for your mistakes, or for your intolerance or bad temper (*'If you had not got me looking for your toy, then I wouldn't have burnt the saucepan!' 'If you had not kept on nagging me about that trip to the shops, I wouldn't have lost my temper with you over this!'*) think carefully about why you seem to feel unwilling to take responsibility for your own behaviour. It might be because you feel pretty bad about yourself. It might be because you cannot tolerate failure or anything less than perfection. Instead of laying blame on others, each time you feel yourself about to do it, just say, *'I'm sorry for what I did'* or, *'Wasn't that silly of me!'* or even something quite neutral such as, *'I wish that had not happened'* and see what effect it has on you and your family. It probably will not be so difficult to carry the responsibility. What, after all, can really happen to you if you do 'own up'? No one is there to punish you except yourself. And the other members of the family will feel respect for you rather than resentment. If you show that it is OK to go pubic about your mistakes, and apologise, you will encourage others in your family to do the same.

Surviving mistakes

Showing that *you* have the strength to admit to, and survive, mistakes encourages children to have the same strength in their dealings with others outside the family. More important, perhaps, is the demonstration that the *relationship* can survive errors. You can approach them again, with your olive branch, to make amends, and you give them the option to do the same in return. Apologising also offers the chance to both give and experience **forgiveness**. If children grow up with the experience of apology and forgiveness within the family, and with an appropriate sense of proportion about the sometimes ridiculous positions we get ourselves into, they will be far better able to negotiate their way through the minefield of relationships in later life.

Different ways of apologising

Different ways of saying sorry include:

- saying it in words

- doing something for your child
- buying something for your child

In words

- *'I'm sorry that I got back later than I said I would.'*
- *'I feel awful that I shouted at you this morning.'*
- *'I wish I hadn't hit you. I feel terrible about it.'*
- *'You did a very naughty thing but I should not have smacked you.'*
- *'I feel horrible inside because I was so horrid to you.'*
- *'I was very silly to get so upset about your messy room.'*

Doing something

Doing something special with and for your child can be more powerful than just saying sorry. It shows that you really mean it. It is a way of repaying them, of evening it out. You might give them their favourite food for tea, read an extra long story at bedtime, or sit and play with them. If saying sorry is hard for you, you do not have to say why you are being extra nice. They will just feel happier because you are giving them special attention, and the resentment will be easier to forget.

However, we cannot do this too often. Too many swings of behaviour, from nasty to very nice without any warning or explanation, are very puzzling and unsettling. It is much better to get used to saying sorry so that our children can understand and predict our behaviour.

Buying something

Giving children time and attention almost always means more to them than buying them something, but *little* surprises given alongside a verbal apology shows that you have given thought to what happened.

Beware apologising too much

There are dangers in apologising too much. The problem lies not with the apology itself, but with the reason for the frequency. If you apologise a lot, you could be conveying uncertainty and guilt. If you consider that you might be doing it too much, it will be worthwhile asking whether you feel uncertain and, if so, why. Children need to feel they can rely on you, the parent. They want you to know your mind. They want you to be sure about what you are doing. They need you to be their rock, a safe and secure place to tether themselves, giving them scope to wander in safety, knowing precisely where you will be and what attitude you will have when they come back. They rely on you for sound guidance. If *you* wander, too, they will not like it. Rather than apologise when you are not sure whether you have done the right thing, it might be better sometimes to *feel* sorry about something but to stay quiet. How can you decide when is the right time to say nothing? This could relate to how much you perceive your child's feelings have been hurt by the action you regret; and by your own judgement about how much is too much.

What happens if you do not apologise?

If someone is clearly in the wrong, and does not apologise for their behaviour, it can cause enormous resentment. Almost certainly, every adult will have some incident from their own childhood etched on their memory when they felt unfairly treated. Children have an acute sense of fairness. They will be fair to you and to others if you are fair to them. Resentment grows and eats away at the good feelings. It is also like a barrier. It grows in thickness and height, gradually cutting off the resentful child from the object of resentment who is causing them distress.

Apologies and you

- If you want to hear them, you need to give them.
- Apologies make you feel better about yourself. They are a statement of honesty and wipe the slate clean.
- If they are given, make sure you accept them.

COMPROMISE

A compromise, like an apology, is often seen as weakness, 'giving in', and the start of a drift towards anarchy. Too often we feel that our authority will be undermined if we do not stick to what we first demand, if we do not rigorously enforce the rules, come what may. But in truth, a compromise shows respect and understanding for the other person's wishes, activities and feelings.

Compromise is:

- a process of giving and taking
- a sign of strength, not weakness
- a Win–Win solution

Not to listen and respond fairly to our children's reasonable complaints, or to what they say they want, is likely to make them resentful and angry. We will end up with less authority in their eyes, and less respect from them. Great damage can be done to the relationship in the name of 'parental authority' when parents dig in their heels regardless of the real importance of an issue.

Compromise is not the same thing as negotiation

Negotiation implies the right to say 'no' and to walk away from agreeing to something.

Compromise involves giving and taking. Some kind of deal is assumed. The only point at issue is what form it will take – who will give way on what. It involves looking at the separate and common interests and seeing if there is a way for each person to get some, most, or all of what they want.

If a compromise is to be a win–win solution and not a win–lose one, it follows that what you are prepared to give is not going to be very important to you – that it does not cost you too much.

***For example**, provided you get the shopping done that morning (non-negotiable), you do not mind whether you do it early or late (area of compromise). Your child has two favourite morning TV programmes, one early and one late. He wants to watch both. But he cannot. There is not the time to get the shopping done in between them. You are prepared to time your shopping so he can watch one, the one he likes best, but not to put it off until the afternoon so he can watch both.*

Compromise is not the same thing as surrender

It is important not to confuse compromising with surrendering. Compromise does not mean that *any* concession will do.

***For example**, in the above situation, it might happen that your child refuses to choose one of the programmes and throws a tantrum. If you then agree, after all, to shop in the afternoon, but say that in return he will have to put away all his toys before bedtime, you would be climbing down. The fact that he agrees to do something else in return does not* make it a win–win compromise.

How to seek a compromise

Some issues are negotiable, some are not. Those issues that are non-negotiable should be identified very clearly from the start with the statement, *'There is no room for negotiation on this. It has to be.'* Where there is room for compromise, it often develops naturally when everybody's separate and common interests are explored. If you do not bother to ask *why* your child wants something to happen differently, or to explain why you need something to happen a particular way, you will never get to common ground, the territory of compromise.

The language you use to reach a compromise can be important.

Don't say	*'I will do this if you will do that.'*
Do say	*'If we do it this way, we can both get what we want.'*

The first option can be seen as manipulative and conditional. This may come back at you later as your child learns the tactics of manipulation. It is better to state that there seems to be a solution in the middle which meets both of our needs.

The dangers in compromising too much

Too much compromise can teach a child to manipulate. The arguments used have got to be relevant. If you justify your demands with layers of arguments, you teach them to try reason after reason. Although it is good for children to be able to reason and muster a good case, they also need to be able to accept when no means no, to learn how to live with the disappointment of not getting their way, and to accept that they cannot always control events.

Six
Words Matter: So Let's Change the Script!
. . . and Turn the 'Put-downs' into 'Puff-ups'

What is a 'put-down'?

A 'put-down' is an *unnecessarily* negative statement which has the effect of making the recipient feel less good about themselves, of damaging their self-respect and belief in themselves and their competence. It is a comment which says something derogatory about **who someone is** or about **what they can do**. It is therefore something which addresses either **personality** or **capability**.

Put-downs:
- humiliate
- lower dignity
- damage self respect
- make someone feel small or unimportant
- make someone feel incompetent
- burst the bubble of confidence
- give someone bad feelings about themselves

Put-downs inevitably create some distance between the giver and the receiver, both because the person on the receiving end is bound to recoil at the sense of insult and humiliation, and because the person who utters the offending comment establishes the space in the very act of putting themselves in judgement over the other.

A put-down is therefore also a 'push-away'. It is a verbal assault. Put-downs can seriously damage relationships and individuals, especially if they are frequent. They can cause resentment and create distance and resistance. When the child grows up, his poor self-image and lack of trust can affect all his subsequent relationships. Someone who is put down a lot will also be less likely to stand up for others because, far from empathising and feeling the same hurt or humiliation, they are more likely to relish the fact that someone else is in the firing line for a change.

Yet put-downs are not always delivered with evil intent. They can become almost involuntary – said without thinking – because we get into set ways of saying things and rarely think about their effect. Our words can become almost predetermined, as if they were scripted in a play.

If we are to establish a good and healthy relationship with our children, and convey to them that we like them and are comfortable with them, it is clear that we have to reduce the number of reprimands we use which undermine them. Deciding to change the script, and write the put-down out of it, does not mean that we can never tell children off. It does mean that we comment on their behaviour in ways which do not damage their self-respect and make them doubt our commitment to them.

Why are children so vulnerable to put-downs?

Deep down, most of us are quite insecure and it is very easy to believe the worst of what someone says about us. Children have fewer opportunities than adults to meet people outside the home who will give them independent feedback about how likeable they are. What is said to them at home, then, will have a significant impact, especially as it will be said by the people they love most in the world. It will need at least three puff-ups to cancel out the damage of one serious put-down.

What is a 'puff-up'?

A 'puff-up' is the opposite of a 'put-down'. Instead of deflating someone's ego, it is a descriptive or affirmative comment which builds up someone's view of themselves and makes them feel good about themselves and what they can do. It will allow their ego to swell a little, to puff up with pride, and give them a warm glow of approval and achievement.

Many people dislike the idea of giving a little boost to their child's ego. It smacks of flattery. They think it might make their child big-headed. However, provided a child realises that his particular abilities do not make him better as a person than others less talented, there is every reason to let him know what he is good at. Unpleasant big-headedness can be avoided as long as 'good at' is not seen to be the same thing as 'better than' in anything other than comparative skill terms.

To guard against inappropriate conceit while encouraging a legitimate pride, we can apply the distinction between the **deed** and the **person** which was raised earlier in the section on 'Praise' (page 97).

- **Value them** for *who they are*, and **praise them** for *what they have done*.
- Ensure that we **value a variety of skills** so that children learn tolerance.
- Teach that '**good at**' means '**different from**', not 'better than'.

Within this framework, children should be able to manage a more competitive environment which stimulates and challenges, and offers the incentive to achieve and improve. Contrary to widespread popular belief, the absence of challenge and competition does not necessarily make children feel happy and unthreatened. Lack of challenge can damage self-esteem just as effectively as too much of the wrong kind of challenge.

How to change the script

Changing how you say things is not very easy. It is helpful to look at it step by step.

Step One ***Feel the impact and effect that put-downs have on children and others.***

Think about the last time someone put you down. **How did it make you feel?** It might have made you feel inadequate, small, angry, like hiding away, wanting to cry, or perhaps you felt defiant, wanting to assert that you did not care. *Why should a put-down make your child feel any different?*

What did it make you want to do? Did it make you want to hurt somebody or something, say something hurtful back, or want to shut yourself away? *Why should it make your child want to do anything different?*

What did you actually do? You might have taken it out on someone else, sent your accuser to 'Coventry', defended yourself verbally, insulted them back, hit them – or done nothing but seethed. *Should your children do anything different?*

Step Two ***Recognise the different types of put-down.***

Criticisms are a form of judgement. A child who is subjected to constant criticism gets the message not only that you are disappointed by her but also that you do not like who she is and what she does. You want her to be different. You want her to do whatever it is in the way *you* would have done it. In other words, you want her to be like you. If you try to turn someone else into yourself, it can mean that you desperately need to love yourself, but do not. Criticism is a means of control. You cannot give someone the space or time to do things their own way. You have to intervene at regular intervals to maintain your control, to mark out your territory.

Strait-jackets are statements about a person which lock them into a personality or a role (*'You always . . .' 'You are just like . . .' 'You will never . . .'*) not allowing them a chance to be different and not giving them the benefit of the doubt. All people, but especially children, develop and change. It is extremely unfair to get fixed ideas about someone and force that role or image on them often in the face of the evidence. Strait-jackets can encourage children to become whatever it is you say they are. They live up to, or down to, their image. The strait-jacket can become a self-fulfilling prophecy.

Strait-jackets come in two forms: *Labels* describe what the child is (*'You are useless, a moron, an idiot, lazy, untidy'*) and what they are not (*'You will never be any good at school, sport, drawing . . .'; 'Why don't you ever . . . tell the truth, do what I tell you, finish anything . . . ?'*). *Comparisons* involve the child being measured against someone else, a brother or sister (*'Ahmed's much . . . cleverer, tidier, more reliable . . . than you'*) a friend (*'Why can't you be honest, like Scott is with his mum?'*) or a parent (*'With that temper, you're going to grow up just like your dad'*). Even where the comparison with a parent is favourable, the child may feel unable to be how she wants to be. First and foremost, she wants to be herself and to have her parents believe the best, not the worst.

Arbitrary behaviour in adults shows to the others affected that their needs are not worth respecting. Unpredictability is a tool to keep others on tenderhooks, to keep them guessing and waiting, making them focus their energies on the volatile character, trying to read the signs for when the next flare-up will be and trying to placate and keep things calm.

Blame, sarcasm and ridicule are all forms of criticism, so the comments above also apply to this type of put-down.

Anger and shouting count as put-downs because they both suggest that the adult is right and the child is wrong. Each of them is a tool of power used by adults. In summary, any tactic which is used as a tool of power and control can be deployed as a put-down.

Step Three

Understand why you might use put-downs.

When we put children down, we usually believe that we are reacting to *their* behaviour. We therefore hold *them* in some way responsible for what we say. If we say nasty things, it is because they have done something nasty. This is a very comfortable way for us to look at our behaviour. It allows us to **avoid responsibility** for what we do. But probably every time we say something there will be another form of words we could have used which would have got the same message across. We do not have to be nasty. We, not they, are responsible for what we say, and what words we use to express our disapproval.

In fact, how we respond in these situations is influenced more by how we feel about ourselves. We put other people down because, for a small moment, **it makes us feel better about ourselves**. Afterwards, we might feel enormously guilty but at the time it makes us feel:

- stronger, superior, and reminds us that we hold some power; in other words, we are in a position to tell off, to pass judgement on another;

- better, just by comparison, because we have made someone feel worse;
- less embarrassed by, and less responsible for, that person's behaviour. Children's behaviour is widely seen as a measure of how 'good' a parent we are. We don't want to seem to accept behaviour which we feel reflects badly on us, particularly when we are in company. We want to say: *'Don't think that* I *am anything to do with this!'* So we distance ourselves from the child by telling him off and putting him down. We care more about what others think of us than what our child thinks of himself.

Sometimes we use put-downs because those are the words our parents used to us. There can be a feeling of comfort in returning to the familiar, however bad we felt when these things were said to us.

Being 'in charge' of our children is often interpreted as being in control. If we feel we are losing that control, we might find it easier to belittle and humiliate our children than to confront the more difficult issue of rediscovering our confidence and reasserting our responsibility and authority, especially if we were put down a lot ourselves as children.

Once we understand why we fall into the habit of using put-downs, we should find it easier to avoid them.

Step Four **Realise afterwards when you have said the wrong thing.**

Nothing can be changed unless you recognise it first.

Step Five **Hear yourself saying it** while you are saying it, when you are in full flood.

'I hear myself saying it but I can't stop myself.' At least the error is recognised. You can always apologise for what you have said and withdraw it, for example: *'I think I went a bit too far then. I didn't mean that.'* Then you should decide

what you *could* have said instead to say what you meant less harmfully – **and speak it**. Practise it, whispered if necessary, but you must get used to what it feels and sounds like to say the new script.

Step Six ***Stop yourself before you begin*** and substitute a more acceptable form of words.

Now that you have practised the alternative words, you know what you can say and it will be easier to slip them in. They may sound strange at first, but it should not be long before you reach the final stage and – most of the time – they come naturally.

Step Seven Finally the reprogramming will be complete and the alternative script will be learned and will come naturally.

Congratulations! You have made it. And you probably feel much better about yourself for having made the change, and therefore in less need to put others down!

Each step taken will be something to be proud of. It will not necessarily be a smooth process. Like children's changes, there can be two steps forward and one step back, particularly when you are feeling stressed or not feeling very confident in yourself. Being realistic, you are unlikely to obliterate completely the hurtful phrases from your repertoire. But if you can cut them down, recognise when you have been horrid and make amends for it, and take every suitable opportunity in between to raise your child's self-esteem, you should have made enough impact to initiate an upward spiral of improving behaviour on both sides.

Some common put-downs follow, with some alternative, neutral ways of expressing the same feelings alongside. Where relevant, the put-down is also presented in its more demeaning question form, to show it forces a child to agree and puts him onto the defensive.

Put-downs which undermine self-esteem

Put-downs	Alternatives
Attaching labels	
You're useless. Why are you so useless? You are so clumsy.	It wasn't so smart to clean your boots without covering the floor. You've got so much going on in your head, you're too busy to look where you're going!
Rejection	
I can't take you anywhere.	I don't like how you behave when we go out. I know you can do better than that.
Why do you always embarrass me?	People don't like children when they behave like that. Don't you like me talking to my friends?
I wish you had never been born.	It can be hard understanding why you do it.
Why don't you go and live with your dad?	We need some cooling off time. Let's go into separate rooms and we'll talk again in 30 minutes.
Threats	
I'll throw you out if . . .	When you behave like that, it makes you hard to live with. What is it you feel isn't going right?
I'll send you away . . .	That behaviour is not acceptable. Do you realise how angry it makes me?
I'll tell your teacher . . .	I don't think you're proud of what's happened. Let's make sure it doesn't happen again.
Instilling a sense of badness	
I'll call the police. You're a rotten apple – that's the truth. You'll end up in prison, I'll bet. Why can't you keep out of trouble?	You know what you did was wrong. Sometimes, I just can't cope, you seem to like getting into trouble. Let's spend more time together. We used to have such fun. What are you doing Saturday?
Lack of respect	
I don't care what you think/want.	I feel very strongly about this and I'm not prepared to negotiate over it.

Why are you always bothering me?	Now's not a good time. I'll listen better after tea.
Deflating	
What's so good about that?	You seem pleased with how you have done.
So and so did better than that.	Did you do your best? Are you pleased with it?
Lack of trust	
Where did you get that from? I can never believe you.	That's smart. Is it new or has someone lent it to you?

What two things do you say?	What can you say instead?
•	•
•	•

Put-downs which undermine competence

Put-downs	Alternatives
I suppose I'll have to do it for you. *Why do I always have to do it for you!*	You've done well so far. Would you like help with the last bit?
Don't carry the milk bottle. You'll drop it.	Keep one hand underneath then it won't slip.
You always give up before you've really tried. *Why do you always give up!*	Next time you'll get a bit further. It's always hard to start with. Frustrating, isn't it?
You'll never learn. *Won't you ever learn!*	These things are always harder than you think. Practice makes perfect!
I had to help out when I was your age. *Why are you so unhelpful!*	I've got a lot on at the moment. I'd love some help – and company.
I was able to cook at your age! *Why aren't you practical!*	Get your radio and help me do supper. You'll pick up some useful tips.
You always lose/forget things. *Why do you always lose things!*	Let's think of some ways to help you keep tabs on your coat/PE kit.

What two things do you say?	What can you say instead?
•	•
•	•

Seven
Discipline, Self-Discipline and Self-Esteem

Discipline is the aspect of child-rearing which causes most parents most heartache. It is also the thing which most parents feel they do not get right. Society, and its values, have both changed to such an extent that many parents either feel out of touch with traditional approaches or feel little sympathy with them, and are very confused about what they should be doing instead. There is tremendous uncertainty about whether, what and how we should discipline, and how we can react to limit bad behaviour without playing power and causing an irreparable rift between parent and child.

Under the combined influence of the American, child-centred attitudes of the sixties, and fuelled by the social freedoms preached in the same era, 'discipline' has become something of a dirty word. It is still largely seen as something negative and unpleasant which acts against the interests of children. Viewed as an oppressive instrument of adult power play and control, interfering with the full self-expression and development of the child's individuality, it became – and to a large extent still is – seen as not just 'unfashionable' but also 'old fashioned'. Yet the replacement, the so-called 'permissive' approach, has not really proved itself to be a practical successor. Parents are beginning to doubt its long-term effectiveness in terms of preparing their children to participate, constructively and contentedly, in society outside the home.

In a recent MORI poll (July 1993) parents were invited to explain the level of crime in Britain today. Just over six people in ten (63%) blamed unemployment. But almost as many (54%) named lack of parental discipline as an important factor. This may not be the correct explanation for rising crime, but parents clearly feel they are failing. It is time to look afresh at what we mean by discipline and to construct an approach which achieves four overall aims.

- It must pave the way for children to **acquire self-discipline**.
- Children must have the space within it to develop **self-esteem**, **self-confidence** and **self-reliance**.
- It must **encourage flexibility and initiative** to prepare children for living in today's fast-changing world.
- Parents must feel comfortable with it and **find it easy to apply**.

What is – or should – discipline be about?

For many people, the word 'discipline' conjures up images of the Victorian patriarch wielding a cane. Discipline is inseparable from punishment, and punishment is closely associated with, if not inseparable from, hitting or beating. Discipline is therefore about power and obedience, and about rule by fear. This is what some people think discipline *should* be like, and it is also the reason so many others went in the opposite direction to reject it. If this is the model we are to reimpose on our children, turning the clock back, we will not give our children the tools to make a success of their lives.

If rule by fear is not an acceptable model of discipline, what is? Is there something in between the traditional, authoritarian style and total permissiveness? What is discipline really about? Why do we need it? If it is so important, will any kind of discipline do? What approach does give young people the right skills to thrive and survive in today's world?

Discipline in its best sense can and should be seen as a positive and constructive force. It is the help adults give to children so they can learn how to control and manage their behaviour. It involves making clear how we expect our children to behave in different situations – setting out behaviour guidelines, or limits and boundaries – restricting and prohibiting certain things, not for the sake of it but to achieve some very important objectives. Discipline is also necessary to:

- keep children safe;
- teach children to think of others, including their parents;
- provide a predictable and therefore secure environment for children to operate in;
- help children develop a constructive independence;
- make clear the difference between acceptable and unacceptable behaviour;
- demonstrate that actions have consequences;
- aid the smooth running of any group, for example, the family or school.

Discipline, therefore, confers practical advantages. It should not be seen as a negative, punitive concept but as a positive and *enabling* tool for creating consistency, predictability, security and the right environment for (as its source, 'disciple', suggests) teaching and learning. It should not rely on, or be about, wielding power: commanding obedience, handing out punishment and maintaining absolute control like a dictator. As explained in Chapter Three, playing power with children teaches them the same game and invites them to copy our, or to think up their own, power responses. All children need boundaries, to help them control and manage their behaviour. But our target should be discipline without dictatorship – discipline based not on power and deference, but on fairness and mutual respect.

What are boundaries?

It helps to start by thinking in terms of the negative – of being 'out of bounds'; beyond, or outside, the boundary is forbidden territory where you are not allowed to tread. Being inside the boundary is safe and allowed. But when psychologists use the concept, they do not use it in a geographical or territorial sense. They are talking about the point at which certain behaviours are allowed and not allowed. It is therefore the meeting point between right and wrong, not in some high moral sense, but what individual parents have decided they want, or do not want, their children to do in particular instances. Boundaries are therefore rules and expectations governing behaviour which create a kind of perimeter fence, or limit, beyond which we do not expect our children to go – but within which they are free to act as they please.

Boundaries as a 'play pen'

Children are safe in a play pen; and they can choose what to play within it. At the beginning they do not know how to, or cannot, climb out. But as they grow, they will realise that they have the skill to escape, and they are rightly proud of this. We trust them not to climb out. When they do, we put them back enough times for them to get the message, until we need to redraw the boundaries and offer a larger play space.

Parental authority and responsibility

Creating boundaries for behaviour within which there is scope for choice, growth and development involves exercising **authority** and **responsibility**.

- We cannot expect children to do what we say without taking *responsibility* for deciding in advance, and stating clearly, what behaviour we expect or will accept.
- We cannot expect them to take the rules seriously if we do not take *responsibility* for monitoring their behaviour so we can comment favourably when they keep within the rules and take action if they regularly ignore them.
- We cannot expect our children to respect and trust us if we have not demonstrated our *authority* by setting an example and by expecting, rather than enforcing, compliance.

You and your partner: the importance of presenting a united front

It helps enormously if you and your partner can agree on what the rules are. A united front is far more convincing, and therefore effective, than a divided one. If you and your partner cannot agree on them all, you can:

- select, say, the four areas which are most important to you both and compromise, if necessary, to agree on this core group;
- share out the lower priority issues between you: *'We do this your way, and that my way'*;
- agree that whoever is 'in charge' at any one time handles any difficulties without interference from the other unless invited.

Any differences of attitude or approach should be discussed in private, and **not** in front of the child unless you feel his interest is immediately at stake. Differences are often exploited, and create divided loyalties for the children which they will find extremely difficult to manage.

You should not expect to get or to have agreement on everything. It is natural that we will have different expectations, based on the different ways we were brought up. Also, sometimes, we get wound up about an issue and go too far. It is important, then, to hear what someone else says about other ways of handling things. This also means that if you disagree with what your partner is doing, *and you think your child's immediate or long-term interests are at stake*, it is vital that you have the confidence to say so and to forget the rule about the united front.

Important things to remember are:

- all children need some boundaries and routines;
- all children should have the experience of certain behaviour being expected of them;
- it is better to have just a few rules, and to stick to them, than too many which are constantly ignored;
- remember the age of your child – *don't set them up to fail* by asking too much of them.

Which style of discipline best meets our objectives?

Everyone has his or her own style of discipline, or parenting. ('Parenting style' amounts to the same thing as discipline style.) Three core styles can be identified:

The **autocratic** style is usually associated with a traditional, adult-centred regime in which there are many, rigid boundaries drawn, without much discussion, around negatives – 'thou shalt not . . .'.

The home tends to be tightly organised, and parental power reigns supreme.

At its best the autocratic household can offer a highly secure regime; but at its worst it can be very arbitrary. New rules can be imposed without warning or without appropriate justification or reference to criteria of fairness, if it suits the adults. It can all too easily develop into a 'Jump when I say so!' power game, the parents checking regularly that they still have a hold on the child and others around them by requiring immediate compliance.

In a home in which there are lots of fixed rules, there is little opportunity for a child to make choices, experiment, make mistakes and therefore to find out about himself. Adults determine what the child is allowed to do. If obedience is valued, the child is accepted only if he is 'good', abiding by someone else's view of what is desirable, and is not accepted for himself. Making mistakes – essential for developing creativity, flexibility and self-reliance – is seen either as not conforming or as failing to come up to standard, and is likely to be punished as unacceptable.

In authoritarian homes, adults get their way regardless of the wishes and interests of the child. Little or no respect is shown for the impact of the rule or decision on the child, or for the child's need for a degree of self-determination. Differences of opinion result in clashes not compromise, and clashes produce resentment and ultimately withdrawal. Children in authoritarian families learn to play the same power game as the parents.

The child raised in such a home may be able to fit in to society. But doing as he is told and only as he is told, fearing authority and punishment, and being unable to exercise initiative will teach him what he can get away with, will hinder the growth of self-discipline and damage the ability to be creative and flexible. This child will be filled with self-doubt and may become authoritarian himself in order to mask this.

The **permissive** style is at the other end of the spectrum. In permissive, child-centred homes, there are no clear boundaries. The child is indulged and calls the shots. The parent has neither power nor authority.

Here, the boundaries constantly change. There is no consistency. The child *will* test the limits and will *always* go for more, trying to find out where the boundaries are. The boundaries shift, and are usually found on each occasion when the adult has finally had enough and goes berserk. The environment can, then, be highly unpredictable and highly charged, and the child will never really know where she stands. The insecurity and confusion will be intensified by the parent switching between the permissive and the autocratic models when they see that 'things have got out of hand' and they need to reassert control, and then switching back again when they cannot keep it up and see that that does not work either.

The child in this home will have far too many choices. She gets what she wants. Far from giving her a healthy sense of autonomy, of being in control of herself and being trusted, she will actually feel she is also in control of the adults. This excessive power will not only make her feel uncomfortable and insecure, it will also teach her little about herself. Getting her own way on most things will not teach her to prioritise or to develop judgement. Seeking out the boundary point where someone finally says 'no' means that she demands things which do not accurately reflect her real wishes or interests. She does not have to decide what is really important to her. Also, not being used to hearing or responding to 'No', she does not experience disappointment.

This child is not encouraged to develop any sensitivity to other people's needs. She thinks only of herself, and learns to manipulate (this is sometimes dressed up more respectably as negotiation) in order to get her way, ignoring objections to her demands.

Fitting in will be hard and the root insecurity generated by floppy boundaries and inconsistency mean that change can be petrifying. Fear of change can numb and paralyse.

The **democratic** approach lies somewhere in between. This offers fewer, firm but flexible boundaries within which there is mutual respect and freedom to explore and to make mistakes. The rules are not just negative but define both rights and responsibilities; and the parent relies much more on natural authority than on the tools of power.

The basic framework is predictable, but there is freedom within the rules, which are not adult-centred. Instead, they define both the rights and the responsibilities of everyone in the social unit. Alterations can be made to the boundaries where appropriate, but only after discussion, and the changes will not, therefore, appear as arbitrary.

There is plenty of scope for choice here, but within clear limits. The choices made available to the child are 'managed' and appropriate both in terms of the child's age and what the parent is prepared to make happen. Choices also make any restrictions elsewhere easier to bear. Through choices and the exercise of priorities, children learn to develop their own rules.

Rights and feelings are acknowledged by both sides. The child therefore not only feels respected but also learns to respect and anticipate the interests of others. Through the process of agreeing who gets what and when, and trading interests, the child learns to *reason* and to *compromise*. Where authoritative decisions are taken, the child can more easily accept that they are taken in his own best interests and knows that in other situations, where it is appropriate, he has an opportunity to state his interests.

This child has to fit in with authority but his own rights have been respected. His environment has been consistent and rule-related but not stiflingly so, with the freedom to express himself and to develop his skills and confidence. Mistakes can be made and, being more secure and confident himself, he is able to manage change and take risks.

'Democratic discipline' clearly scores best. It is better able to supply the conditions conducive to the development of self-esteem, self-confidence, self-reliance, and flexibility. The chart opposite provides a summary of this analysis.

Does 'democratic discipline' also deliver the first of the four objectives – good self-discipline?

Discipline styles and the development of self-discipline

One of the main purposes of raising children in a framework of discipline is to encourage self-discipline. Parents cannot have influence for ever. At the end of the day, children have to become responsible for themselves. What is the connection between discipline and self-discipline? Is it possible to develop self-imposed discipline later without early discipline imposed by adults? Will any kind of discipline experience produce self-discipline? If not, what, in particular, is it about early experiences of discipline which help us to develop self-discipline? What is the connection between discipline and morality? This is a book for parents, not moral philosophers, but we need to have some idea of the answers in order to act in a manner which achieves

Diagram 1. Discipline styles and the development of self-esteem

Scope for ☞	Consistent *versus* arbitrary environment	Choice and independence	Compromise and consultation	Parental power play and control	Nagging and criticism
Leads to ☞	Security	Self-esteem, confidence	Mutual respect	Inequality	Self-doubt
Styles of Discipline 'AUTOCRATIC' Traditional style, rigid Adult-centred 'Thou shalt not.' Tightly organised home *Many tight boundaries*	At best, a consistent and secure environment where everyone knows their place At worst . . . very abritrary. Beware the drill sergeant: 'Jump when I say so!'	Very little choice 'Do what I say you can do.' Child has less chance to find out who she is Child accepted only if she sticks to the rules	Very little consultation Clash rather than compromise, leading to resentment Little chance to show trust or respect	Very high control, and the potential for abuse Little reference to the merits or justice of rules or decisions Child learns to play the same tricks of power and control	DANGER! Lots of rules can mean lots of failures at living by them . . . for both parents and children
'DEMOCRATIC' Freedom within rules Rules define the rights and responsibilities of everyone *Fewer, flexible but firm boundaries*	Basic structure or framework predictable Alterations possible, discussed and *not* arbitrary	Plenty, but within limits Appropriate and managed choice Child accepted for who she is	Plenty, within limits Rights and feelings are acknowledged Child learns to accept others' boundaries Child learns to reason and compromise	You are their equal but you are the adult Parent is a figure of *authority* ie holds *legitimate* power Less chance of abuse if child allowed to challenge on merits	Should be less criticism Fewer rules, clearly stated Child given space *to be themselves*, and *to make mistakes*, within the boundaries
'PERMISSIVE' Child-centred, indulgent Give in a lot *No clear boundaries*	No consistency Highly unpredictable 'The boundary is when I flip my lid!' Child tests the limits always goes for more Child never knows where she stands	Too much choice. Child never has to prioritise and judge Child given too much power = insecurity	Very little Child used to getting her own way Not sensitive to *your* rights and needs Child learns to manipulate and negotiate	Parent has neither power nor authority Child is in control and holds the cards	No clear expectations, therefore lots of nagging and criticism You step in when it goes too far . . . and it always does!

the outcome we want.

There seem to be three components to self-discipline. These are: *habit*, or 'routinised' behaviour (doing things such as hanging your coat up when you come in or always doing homework before TV, without taking conscious decisions); *self-interest*, or being able to do without immediate pleasures in order to achieve greater personal rewards later (such as studying for exams); the ability to make *moral judgements* – to appreciate the value of doing things for the benefit of other people, individually or collectively, even if it is not in your own interest – and to develop a personal code of behaviour.

Self-discipline therefore requires that we:

- think ahead, and **appreciate the wider consequences** of different actions;
- **accept responsibility** for our actions;
- have a clear idea about **what is good for ourselves and others**;
- are able to **make our own rules**;
- are able to stick to the rules, made by ourselves or others, and be sufficiently focused to **see things through**;
- trust our own **judgements**;
- are able to accept **disappointment**.

For all these things to happen, we need to have a clear and positive sense of ourselves – good self-esteem. As has been argued, only some forms of discipline foster good self-esteem. 'Discipline', of itself, is not enough. Having good personal and work habits or routines helps, but does not go far enough. 'Knowing', in the sense of being told, the difference between right and wrong is not enough either: 'knowing' does not mean we will *choose* to do right, and true self-discipline means that we should be able to evaluate such things for ourselves. But to have self-discipline we do need experience of 'task commitment' or 'stickability', of seeing something through to the end. We also need to have had other people's approval and support for our judgements so that we begin to trust ourselves and do things because we want to do them, not because someone else has told us to and will be pleased if we comply.

Which form of discipline is best at producing self-discipline?

Children must have some experience of routines, but they must not be dominated and taken over by these. They need to have the consequences of their behaviour made clear to them, and to take responsibility for what they decide to do. They need adult help in meeting long-term commitments, so they experience the pleasure of working towards and achieving a goal which minimises the experience of failure – *'stickability'*. Finally, children must have an environment of mutual trust and respect in which to develop their own appropriate judgements, and be trusted and approved of for these. The traditional model of strict discipline cannot provide all these experiences; neither can the 'soft' options.

The winner, once again, is democratic discipline – offering the right mix of rules, routines, guidance, support, commitment, freedom and choice.

Putting democratic discipline into effect

Having looked at three of our overall objectives, we must now consider the last. Is it easy to apply?

The discipline contract

There are two parties to the good behaviour agreement – you, and your child. It can be presented as a contract. We should not expect children to behave well if we do not meet them at least halfway. To make discipline work for you, you might consider the following code of behaviour as a way to fulfil *your* side of the contract:

Be fair	Being fair is the best way to avoid resentment and to gain your child's respect. Don't make her suffer for your bad mood, and keep things in proportion.
Be clear	State the rules and the likely consequences of breaking them clearly and in advance. Think ahead. If you are failing to plan, you are planning to fail! If you have not made the rule clear beforehand, let the issue go and apply it next time.
Be firm	Whatever rules you make stick to them, eight or nine times out of ten, but room for flexibility is important.
Be positive	Praise and rewards work better than punishment. Let your child know you've noticed when she has tried hard, and give her plenty of cuddles.
Be creative	Try to divert her if you see trouble brewing – 'a confrontation avoided is better than a battle won'; compromise; or move your special vase to safety.
Be sensitive	Remember her age, and don't ask for more than she can deliver; apologise if you get it wrong.
Give time	Don't let bad behaviour be the only way of getting your attention.
Offer choices	This will make any restrictions in other areas easier to accept.

Punishment and discipline: the link

Discipline, as we have seen, is not the same thing as punishment. Setting out guidelines is a very different process from meting out punishments. Children almost always respond better to positive comments about their behaviour than to punishment. However, punishment can be necessary on occasions because:

- it teaches cause and effect. It helps children to realise that their actions have consequences – for other people and for themselves;
- it makes children take responsibility for their behaviour. If they take the decision to do something, knowing it to be wrong, they must shoulder that responsibility and be prepared to accept the penalty;
- it reinforces the lines which we draw between right, or acceptable, and wrong, or unacceptable, behaviour. It shows that we mean business.

Punishment without humiliation. Why is this important?

The punishment which we use should never humiliate a child. If we punish children in a way which also humiliates them, we are using an unnecessary degree of power. Humiliation undermines the person, damages self-esteem and leads inevitably to resentment, antagonism, hostility and, ultimately, to withdrawal from the relationship.

Punishment which humiliates a child does not work long-term. It is self-defeating. A child who feels unfairly treated will find other ways to get his own back, even if he does what you force him to do at the time. It will teach a child the importance of not getting caught, and nothing about how to accept responsibility and develop self-control and self-restraint.

Isn't all punishment humiliating?

Punishment need not be humiliating. It need not belittle, hurt, physically or emotionally degrade, or otherwise undermine the person in any way. It need not be physical. There are many alternatives to smacking which are far less severe, and much more appropriate to the kind of negative behaviour which young children display.

To smack or not to smack?

Smacking is almost never the best way to stop a child doing something *again*. It may stop him then and there, but this should not always be your target. If you deal only with the immediate incident, it means that you are repeatedly involved in reacting and punishing, each time it occurs. It gets you nowhere. Punishing children in that way is unhelpful. It teaches them how to *avoid getting caught*. It also completely fails to teach them *how* to change their behaviour, to understand *why* it might be in their interests to change it, or to give them any good reason for *wanting* to change it.

'But Mum, you're supposed to look after me!'

These immortal words were said by a distraught and disbelieving two-year-old on being smacked for the first time. She clearly felt utterly betrayed. The first assumption of her life – that the person on whom she depended totally for survival would always protect her from harm and deliver care – had been shattered. Her trust had been thrown into question. She ran to her mother, who had delivered the smack, for consolation for her grief.

Her feelings, if not her words, will be repeated within every child in every similar situation. To hurt your own child is something we are all tempted to do on occasion. But it is something a child will never understand because, in their eyes, you are supposed to love and care. If you, the parent, are not 'on their side', who else will be? It marks the beginning of a rift which will get increasingly difficult to heal. If a child thinks you do not care for her, why should she care about what you think?

Smacking usually makes things worse

Smacking is also best avoided because it does not work. Many children use bad behaviour either to get attention or to gain control. Punishment *is* that desired attention and, by making us stop what we are doing to give the punishment, is the process of regaining control. Sometimes, then, punishment will actively encourage children to reoffend.

Smacking is an act of power. It might frighten a child into submission but the child is likely to get his own back some other way. For every put-down there is a pay-back. Smacking fuels the power battle. It rarely ends it.

Smacking does not usually 'fit the crime'

Smacking is usually, though not always, done on impulse. It is hard to control the force of the blow when we are at breaking point. Often it is 'the last straw', a relatively minor thing, which causes us to lash out. Smacking, then, almost never fits the crime. It happens when we 'go over the top'. When any kind of punishment is out of proportion to the offence, a child will feel ferociously angry and resentful. Her first desire will be either to get even or to withdraw.

If we smack when we are in full control, we still have to think whether to hit and hurt even mildly is the right response to negative behaviour. The only circumstance in which it seems justified to smack a child is to stop them immediately from doing something which is likely to hurt or endanger them significantly more, and when there is not the time to explain or to deal with it gently.

Smacking is arbitrary

Impulse means that we do not plan it. If we cannot predict our own behaviour, our children certainly cannot. Our lashing out is unexpected, arbitrary and, to a child, usually completely incomprehensible; causing more anger and resentment.

Punishment options which avoid physical hurt

There are plenty of alternatives to physical punishment which many parents find more effective than smacking:

- withdrawal of privileges: e.g., going out with friends (being 'grounded'), staying up later at the weekends, sweets;
- restricted use of television, computer, bicycle or other valued activity;
- removal of a favourite toy;
- withdrawal of pocket money for a limited period;
- sending the child to their room;
- send to a 'cooling off' place which is different from their bedroom. It could be the corner of a room, a particular chair, or halfway down the hall or up the stairs;
- send to bed early;
- a verbal telling off.

The punishment contract

Be clear Give clear, advance warning of what the likely punishment will be. If you have not made things clear in advance, it is better to let the incident pass and clarify the rules for next time.

Be fair — Ensure the punishment fits the crime: that it is reasonable, appropriate, and not out of proportion to it.
Wherever appropriate, agree the punishments with your child in advance, so they are seen to be reasonable and are accepted.

Be sensitive — Make it clear that it is the behaviour that is unacceptable, not them: *'That was a stupid thing to do!'* not *'You are so stupid!'*

Be brief — Apply the punishment as soon as possible after the offence and complete it quickly. *'Spend half an hour in your room'* is better than *'You will miss your favourite TV programme for the next three weeks.* However justified that kind of penalty seems at the time, delays and time to replay and reinvent the incident allow resentment to take root.

Be loving — Forget the incident once the punishment is over (easier said than done, but try) and give her a reassuring cuddle to show that you still love her.

Be focused — Do not pile on complaints about other behaviour at the same time. They are irrelevant to the issue at hand; they will send negative messages to the child about how you feel about her; they will act as fertile ground for resentment.

Be firm — Apply the punishments consistently, so she knows what to expect.

All forms of punishment should be used as little as possible

- The more we punish, the more we tell our child that she is 'bad'.
- The more we give her this message, the more she will think that we do not like her.
- The more she sees herself as 'bad', the more she is likely to live up to the image and behave in bad ways, eventually relishing the notoriety

and remaining uninfluenced by the escalating punishments.

- The more we convince her we do not like her, the less she will try to please and behave as we wish.
- The more she gives up trying to please, the less chance we have of successfully changing her behaviour.
- The more we damage her self-esteem, the more likely she is to 'put-down' others, which may eventually get her into trouble with the law.

Think first! Before you punish, think about whether the behaviour which has annoyed you was an accident, the result of thoughtlessness or mischievousness, or intentional bad behaviour. *Most people behave best in a happy, tolerant and understanding atmosphere in which they feel liked and approved.*

Why do we find it difficult to say 'No'?

Saying 'no' to children is not always easy or pleasant. Sometimes, it is very hard work, and we cannot face the struggle. Most of us at some time will find ourselves saying 'yes' when we know we should have said 'no'. Some people almost never say 'no'. But the funny thing is that the more you are prepared to say 'no', and mean it and enforce it, the less you have to use it. Children get the message. Parents who have to say 'no' for most of the day will probably admit that they are not enforcing it. They give in too soon, so children get a mixed message about what they are and are not allowed to do. There are many reasons why we find it difficult to say 'no'. However, there are some common patterns which we all display at some time or other. Have a look at the list below. Do you recognise any one, or more than one, of the reasons applying specially to you?

- We want to protect our child from the 'pain', or discomfort, of disappointment.
- We want to protect ourselves from facing his feelings of anger or disappointment.
- We want to avoid the responsibility of taking a decision about an issue.
- We want to avoid apparently being in a position of power or control.
- We want to keep the peace and fear the row, or other consequences, which may follow.
- We need our child's approval, want to be his friend, and fear his rejection.
- We want to keep the times we are with our child free from conflict.

We can get the necessary strength, confidence and authority to say 'no' when it matters by understanding these reasons more fully.

Protecting your child from the pain of disappointment

Of course, it hurts to see those we love suffer, but mild or modest discomfort and disappointment are facts of life. Children will be better equipped to cope with the realities of life if they experience and learn to manage disappointment, which we often see as pain, especially that of not always getting their own way. This does not mean that we should go out of our way to expose them to pain. It does mean that being the cause of their disappointment is not something we need to feel guilty or ashamed about. Being used to accepting 'no', and realising that they can survive the disappointment, makes them stronger in the face of adversity and also gives them a better idea of which 'wants' are really important to them. Going without from time to time helps to develop both a sense of priorities and a sense of identity.

Protecting ourselves from our child's feelings of anger or disappointment

We often avoid saying 'no' to protect ourselves from having to respond to our children's negative feeling. As parents, we are used to 'making them feel better'; but how can we do this without 'giving in' and sending the feelings away or preventing them in the first place? If we have in some way *caused* the anger or disappointment, what do we do when they display it?

- Stay there.
- Be there.
- Say nothing.
- Talk with touch.

Avoiding the responsibility of taking a decision about an issue

Sometimes we avoid saying 'no' because it involves us in taking a decision about the rights and wrongs of an issue and taking responsibility for that decision afterwards. It is easier to say 'yes', particularly if we don't find it easy to make decisions. Saying 'no' puts the burden on us to have a reason for the refusal, and that involves both thinking the issue through and remaining committed to that decision. If we cannot think of two good reasons for taking that line, then we should at least question the fairness and reasonableness of that decision. We should not always expect to have to supply the reasons to our children. However, as a safeguard and for their benefit, we would do well to check our reasoning and sense of fairness from time to time.

Avoiding apparently being in a position of power and control

Some people love to play power. Other people hate it. For perhaps political or ideological reasons, they hate to be in a position to control and limit the behaviour of others, even their own children. They believe that saying 'yes' allows children to control their own lives; while saying 'no' amounts to inappropriate and illegitimate interference.

Fearful of the row, or other consequences, which may follow

If you find yourself often avoiding saying 'no' because you are frightened of the power battle or retaliations which will follow if you do, it is time to ask yourself two questions.

- *'Have I got myself into a power-type relationship with my child and, if so, why?'*
- *'Am I not in reality being blackmailed by a threatened emotional backlash?'*

If the answer to either of these questions is 'yes', then you have to ask yourself two further questions.

- *'Who is in charge?'*
- *'Who should be in charge?'*

Needing approval, and fearing rejection

Some parents find it hard to say 'no' because they are afraid their child will not like them if they do not give them what they ask for. They need to be liked and need to feel that the child is their friend, and also to believe that their child also sees them as a friend.

The parent who needs the approval, or friendship, of their child to improve their own sense of self-esteem is giving that child a large and very difficult burden which she should not be asked to carry. For that child, the parent will not be that necessary constant factor, offering guidance and security. Instead, the parent will bend with the whim of the child, passing over to the child responsibility for the parent's happiness. In such relationships, the child is likely to be rejected and made to feel guilty if she exposes any of the feelings of anger and even hatred which go hand in hand with childhood love. It is, however, important that children realise that loving and hating is part and parcel of growing up. Both emotions should be accepted.

Wanting to keep the times you are together free from conflict

It is very hard for a parent who does not spend much time with their child to start being tough and causing upset. It is only natural that you want to keep those precious moments free from conflict. Separated fathers are known to spoil their children rotten when it is their weekend 'on'. Working mums who arrive home near bedtime find it hard to resist the pleas and ploys for more time and attention. Children have a way of knowing about the weak spot, and they usually exploit it for all it is worth – which is usually quite a lot.

But giving in, or being soft, is not in their best interest.

Conclusion

Children flourish within an ordered framework of clear expectations and boundaries which offers the scope for mutual trust and respect alongside structure, consistency and commitment. If we return to the Victorian patriarch and a punitive, or rule-governed, model of discipline, not only will we increase feelings within our children of rejection and resentment but we will not give them the experiences which are necessary for them to develop confidence, flexibility and apply self-discipline. Our society will be no better for it, and neither will our children.

Eight
Commitment

Much of what children need in order to grow up secure and happy, and to be strong enough in themselves to be able to give to others, can be summed up in the word '**commitment**'. Children need to feel that someone has both *made a commitment* to them, and continues to *demonstrate* that commitment, consistently.

Making a commitment to something or somebody is usually understood to mean:

- taking on *responsibility* for that thing or person;
- *binding oneself to* someone;
- acknowledging a *sense of duty*;
- *seeing it through*.

When you have a child, you take on a commitment. It is a significant and demanding commitment. You are both responsible for and to that child. You bind yourself to him or her, and it is inevitable that this will be at some, possibly considerable, cost to yourself. A commitment is, according to the dictionary, an 'engagement that restricts freedom of action'. It reduces your freedom. It requires that you put the child's needs before your own – not always, but enough to let him realise that he can rely on you to have his major needs met.

Showing commitment implies:

- loving
- cherishing
- caring
- keeping safe
- being interested
- being there
- offering support

With commitment, children feel valued and welcomed. Without it they feel neglected, abandoned, bereft and alone. If the adults, who *made* him, appear not to care, it will be very hard for any child to develop a sense of self-respect or pride in who he is. A child's self-esteem relies crucially, then, on whether he believes and *perceives* that his parents are committed to him.

How children interpret commitment

Commitment is demonstrated when parents:

- *are there to ask* their child about his life, at home and at school;
- are willing to *see things from the child's point of view*;
- make sure their child is *appropriately fed and clothed*;
- are *tolerant* of the stages and traumas of growing up;
- give their child *rights* at the same time as responsibilities;
- *show respect* for their child.

Commitment is perceived as absent, by implication, when parents:

- *are not at home much* to be with their child;
- are at home but *are not sufficiently interested to play with or talk* to him, to be told about his

life or his day;

- *separate or divorce,* Unable to understand the subtleties of adult relationships until near maturity, the raw message children receive when their parents split up, unless there is obvious violence, is that the departing parent cannot have loved them enough to want to stay with them. (In a television discussion of divorce on the *Kilroy!* programme, many of the young participants believed that their parents had not tried hard enough to save the relationship. Most of them had a very inadequate understanding of why their parents' relationship had failed);
- *disappear from the scene altogether* and lose touch with the child;
- *find a new partner,* and transfer some loyalty and commitment to the new relationship. It is inevitable that at the beginning the 'friend' will be seen as an 'interloper' whose own commitment to the child is likely to be negligible by comparison. If there is a conflict of loyalties, someone has to win or lose, and the child will feel very vulnerable.

What is the effect of uncommitted parenting?

If a child has any reason to doubt the commitment of either parent, he can feel so vulnerable and so full of self-doubt as to be unable to trust, or to commit himself subsequently to, anything or any other relationship. To be able to commit to something or somebody, you have to be able to give and to lose something of yourself to it, to identify with it and to say yes, I am like you, or I believe in you, or in that. You have to know yourself. But for people who have not experienced commitment from their parents, this is really hard.

They will be so well-defended against the possibility of further rejection that they will be extremely wary of giving. (Or, alternatively, they will rush into ill-considered relationships or early motherhood in search of love and commitment, mindless of the consequences for existing or future children.) They will feel that nobody else will want them if their own parents have not shown, to their satisfaction, that they were wanted. And they will be reluctant for anybody or any organisation to take, or expect, anything from them.

The greatest danger comes when people who have not experienced commitment find it difficult, in their turn, either to make or demonstrate a commitment to the children they bring into the world. The damaging pattern can then be repeated. If we do not have the experience of committed parenting, we will be less likely to be able to have, manage or sustain mutually fulfilling relationships which require tolerance, resilience, a strong sense of self, and deep reserves of love, giving and forgiveness. With so little confidence, the process not just of giving and sacrifice, but also of having a firm idea of where to draw the boundaries and what guidance to offer, becomes much more difficult. The problem is not lack of morality in any religious sense, but lack of emotional maturity and human caring.

Discipline, consistency and commitment

Discipline and consistency go hand in hand. There is no point in having rules and regulations if they are not consistently applied. The great advantage of rules and boundaries is that issues do not have to be argued about every time. Consistently applied, they lose their contentiousness and create peace and security. Responsibility for the rules, and any departures from them, is clearly taken by the adult. Consistent application of rules, and of punishments where the rules have been infringed, requires a parent to be involved in the comings and goings and activities of their child. Monitoring behaviour requires a commitment. It is not easy to do. It is far easier to avoid the confrontation, opt out and get on with your own life than to make sure your child does not get away with something which infringes rules. But if you do opt out, the hidden message for your child might be that you do not care about him. Lack of consistency and clear rules defining both rights and responsibilities, therefore, sends deeper messages.

Security comes from certainty and consistency equals commitment:

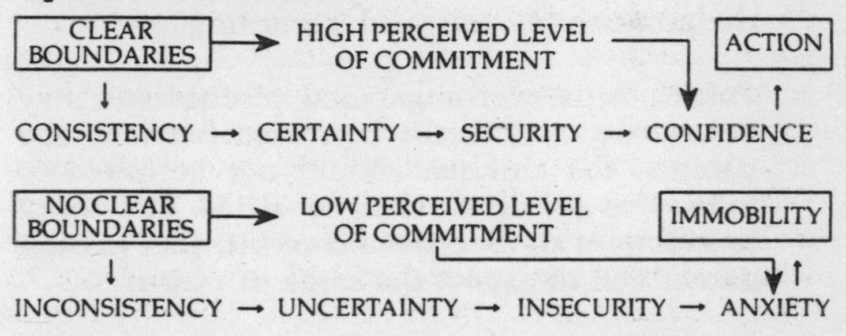

Separation, divorce and commitment

Separation or divorce is a painful process for everyone involved, especially children. It is rarely undertaken without a considerable amount of thought. When parents do decide to go their separate ways, there is much that they can do to make the experience less painful for children.

> ***First***, and foremost, it must be made very clear to them that their parents' difficulties have nothing to do with them. They must not be allowed to take on any feeling of responsibility or blame for the break up.

Second, children must be reassured that both of their parents still love them, and will be continuing as active parents – being there for them – for as long as the children need them. That relationship will not change. We should not forget that in times of stress, children need the security of their parents' love even more.

Third, children should not be kept in the dark, or lied to, about what is happening. Respecting their right to know about things which directly affect them will help them to manage the changes, to keep a sense of control, and to feel loved and respected by their parents – a sign of the promise of continued 'parenting'.

Fourth, whatever anger and resentment may be overtly or covertly expressed between the parents, the children should not be asked to take sides and divide their loyalties. They need to maintain an unfettered commitment to each parent and to expect the same in return.

Fifth, children need opportunities to express their concerns and feelings about what is happening.

Sixth, as many routines as possible should be maintained, to preserve some security during the difficult period of adjustment.

There is no point in bemoaning the rate of relationship breakdown. Relationships will continue to fail and parents will continue to separate. It is far more constructive to focus social comment on the need for parents to accept that the end of their relationship does not, and should not, mean the end of being an active and reliable parent for their children who will continue to have a profound need to be cherished. Throughout the process of moving apart, and for the years of childhood remaining, what really matters is for each parent to demonstrate, unswervingly, a continuing commitment to each child to preserve his or her self-esteem.

Other areas of personal commitment

We have looked at the issue of commitment, or the lack of it, in relationships. But there seem to be consequences in three other areas where people enter adulthood without a sense of belonging or being wanted.

These areas of commitment are:

- tasks
- ideas
- organisations

Commitment to tasks

In many ways, commitment to tasks – what we might call 'stickability' – is more important than commitment to relationships. Those who find it hard to see a job or task through to the end, even when the task is one they set themselves, will have to live with disappointment, frequent failure, low achievement and probably self-hate. It can become a vicious circle in which one failure feeds the next, because they end up not believing in themselves and not even trying.

Task commitment is an important element in self-discipline. Even when the going gets tough, with self-discipline we can keep to our target. Helping our children when they are young to achieve their own aims and those imposed by others, for example the school, teaches them how to see something through. It shows them the pleasure they can get from achieving. They will also enjoy our approval of their effort. They can then become self-motivated. Our interest is a sign of our commitment to them. If we show no encouragement or interest, why should they bother?

Commitment to ideas

Ideas, beliefs and opinions are expressions of ourselves. When we have low self-esteem we do not have such a clear idea of who we are and often do not know what to think. We may therefore be very reluctant to commit to a view in case we want to change it later, either because our view of ourselves may change, or because we do not want to accept the long-term implications of that view. Being unsure, we may also be susceptible to the influence of others around us. If our social group changes, our views might change, too. Someone who is feeling vulnerable may ask themselves: *'Does this idea fit with who I think I am at the moment?'*

Commitment to organisations

Organisations have identities. They also make demands on their members. To commit to an organisation, we have to be able to do two things. First, we have to identify with it and accept that we 'belong' and are similar to other people within it. In other words, we have to have a clear view of ourselves and be willing to lose some of that identity to become one of a crowd. Second, we have to be prepared to give when and if any demands are made. Whether the organisation is educational, job-related or voluntary, someone with good self-esteem is likely to find it easier to conform and commit than someone who is vulnerable.

Sometimes, of course, people with a poor sense of themselves will respond very differently. Instead of holding themselves back from organisations, they will do the opposite. They will seek identity and security in a career or institution which offers them a total way of life. They hand themselves over to the organisation and take comfort from the fact that all major decisions are taken for them.

Commitment and government

Government will have to play its part. It cannot expect full parental commitment if it does not recognise the challenges this involves and demonstrate its commitment with proper support for families. Parenting does not happen in a social or political vacuum. While poverty, of itself, does not mean family failure, the wider context of society today puts sometimes intolerable pressures on those trying to raise children with decency.

We need to re-define and re-discover commitment in parenting. This message is not very easy for parents who are either seduced by the potent temptations of social, personal and material freedom or ground down by the challenge of daily existence in pauperised and crime-torn areas. 'Positive parenting' requires a new contract of commitment from everyone with an interest in improving the overall quality of our society and the quality of life for our children: from government, from the wider community, as well as from parents.

Nine
Conclusion: 'Positive Parenting' and the Positive and Negative Behaviour Circles

The 'good enough' parent

As I have stressed throughout, having self-esteem is crucially important because it impacts on so much of our life – the quality of our relationships, our ability to know our own minds, our willingness to try new things and expand our horizons, and how we deal with life's disappointments. How we feel about ourself influences how we behave towards others, both adults and children. Understanding the common behaviour patterns associated with both low and high self-esteem, seeing that hurt can be done when it goes wrong, and realising how good you and your child will feel when it goes right, will contribute to your finding a new sense of direction in your parenting.

Diagrams 2 and 3 (see pages 188 and 191) illustrate the relationship dynamics set in motion when you feel either good or bad about yourself. The parent is represented in the small circle in the centre. The child is the outer circle. When people are feeling good, there is a tendency to initiate the behaviour patterns and responses shown in the 'positive circle' (Diagram 2) and reproduce those good feelings in those they live with. When people are feeling low and self critical, there is a tendency to set the bad patterns in motion using techniques of power reinforcement and control, and create those same bad feelings in others, as shown in the 'negative circle' (Diagram 3). These diagrams represent summaries of all the issues raised in this book. And they reinforce the positive message that it is possible to understand, manage and adapt our behaviour, and move between the circles, regardless of our own childhood experiences, in order to give our children a firm foundation for a fulfilled and happy life.

The diagrams show that we do not *have* to get locked into a negative cycle of passing on our inadequate feelings to our children. It is not a simple process of the child observing and actively copying self-doubt. If that were the case, it would, indeed, be difficult to break the pattern. By being a more complex process than that, by involving the use of social techniques of power and control, and by subtly putting people down so the initiator can feel good, if momentarily, by comparison, it gives us the opportunity to become aware of what we do and to step in and stop ourselves – at least some of the time. Of course, we become quite set in our ways. Of course, some of the responses and techniques we adopt involve echoes from our own childhood. But if we believe that these early experiences somehow control us, and are part of our blue-print, we might give up trying to change from the start, believing it to be a hopeless or endless challenge. We do not need the psychiatrist's couch and a fat bank balance to inspect and identify the very common ways all human beings cope with the threat of equality and the apparent safety of apparent power.

Diagram 2

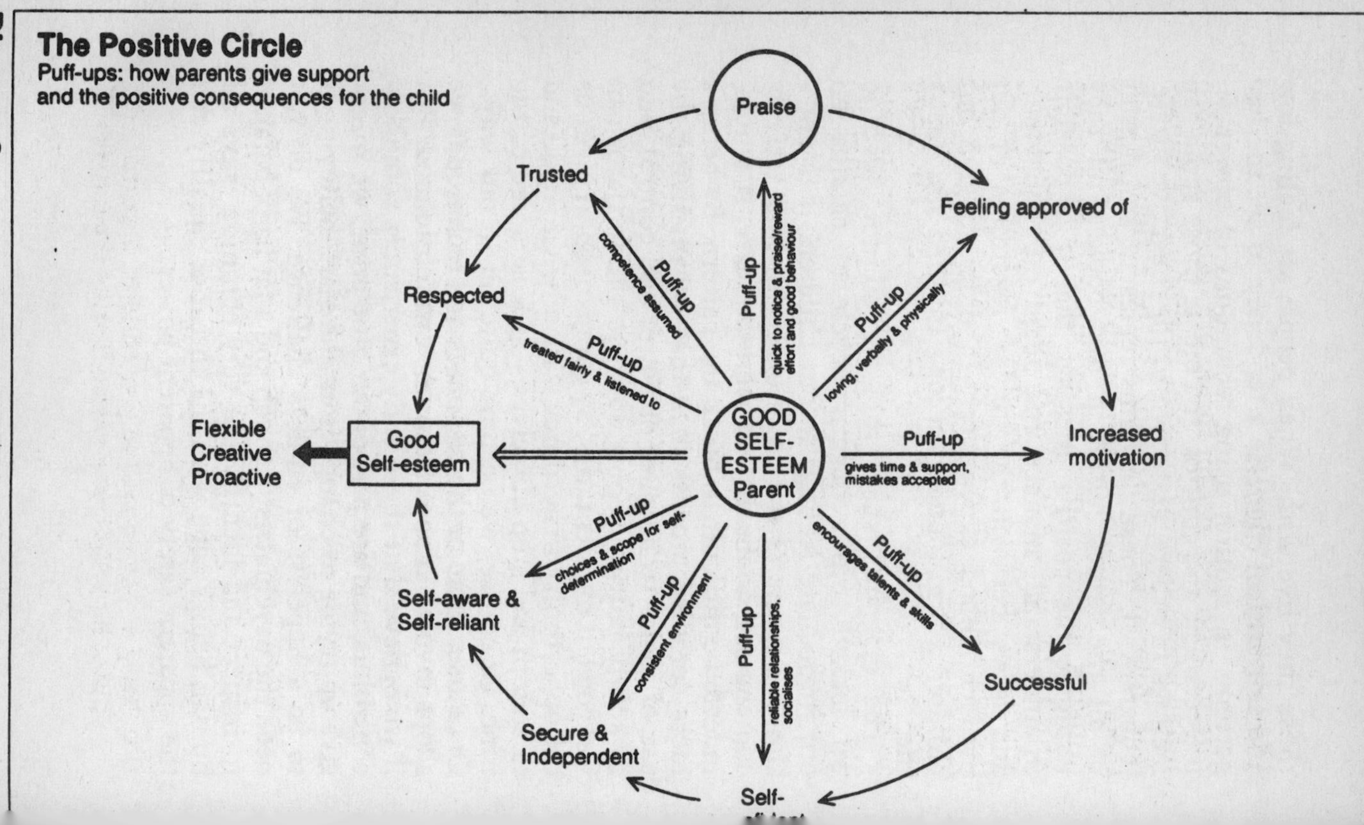
The Positive Circle
Puff-ups: how parents give support
and the positive consequences for the child
Praise
Trusted
Feeling approved of
Respected
Increased motivation
Successful
Self-
Secure & Independent
Self-aware & Self-reliant
Good Self-esteem
Flexible
Creative
Proactive
GOOD SELF-ESTEEM Parent
Puff-up
quick to notice & praise/reward effort and good behaviour
Puff-up
loving, verbally & physically
Puff-up
gives time & support, mistakes accepted
Puff-up
encourages talents & skills
Puff-up
reliable relationships, socialises
Puff-up
consistent environment
Puff-up
choices & scope for self-determination
Puff-up
treated fairly & listened to
Puff-up
competence assumed

The positive circle

Parents who feel strong inside are quick to notice and to praise and reward good, or appropriate behaviour. Appropriate behaviour can be actions which show, for example, kindness, initiative, effort or thinking ahead. 'Good' behaviour will be actions which you have specifically sought, for example, folding pyjamas in the morning, coming home at the agreed time, or sitting at the main table while everyone eats. What is important is that the child's efforts are *noticed* (not because you are checking on him but because you have time for him and are not self-absorbed) and *commented on*, so that he gets some positive feedback.

- **Praise**, combined with physical and verbal demonstrations of love, helps children to feel approved.
- If parents give children **time**, and show interest in what they do, it increases their **motivation** or willingness to work at something, because they do it in part to please their parents. Showing that you think something is important will help your child to attach the same value to the enterprise, whether it is schoolwork, friendships or a leisure activity.
- Opportunities to develop skills and talents will help children to develop **self-confidence** and self-awareness.
- Knowing yourself will help you not only to clarify the kind of regime you want for your children but also to enforce it consistently. **Consistency** demonstrates commitment and creates a secure and predictable environment. Having the strength to say 'No' in the process of enforcing the boundaries consistently reinforces that **security**.
- Being strong enough to give children opportunities for **self-determination**, letting them make

choices about appropriate things, allows them to develop self-reliance.

- Assuming competence, but giving children a safe space within set limits to experiment and make mistakes, shows **trust**.
- Acknowledging children's rights to be heard and treated fairly demonstrates **respect**.

Children who feel approved of are aware of their special skills and talents, are trusted and respected, are confident and independent: are children with good self-esteem.

The negative circle

The dynamics at work in the negative circle, in which a parent is trapped for a time by his or her poor self-image and feels better only when using power in a manner which puts someone down, operate in the opposite direction. We all know that when we have had a bad day or are very tired, we tend to 'take it out' on someone else. Why do we seem to need to do this, and what form does it usually take?

- When we feel vulnerable, we often get rid of our own feelings of inadequacy by **blaming** our children for our own or for general mistakes and mishaps in order to protect our fragile self. But this is very unfair. Wherever blame is placed upon children, children will feel guilt and disapproval. Inappropriate blame is a form of destructive criticism which will, eventually, cripple the recipients and render them incapable of testing themselves, of reaching out or going forward.
- When we feel low, we also tend to emphasise children's **failures** and **mistakes**. We are either simply less tolerant of mistakes at these times, or we can begin to feel let down by them, or even responsible for them. This makes us feel uncomfortable and perhaps guilty, so we again

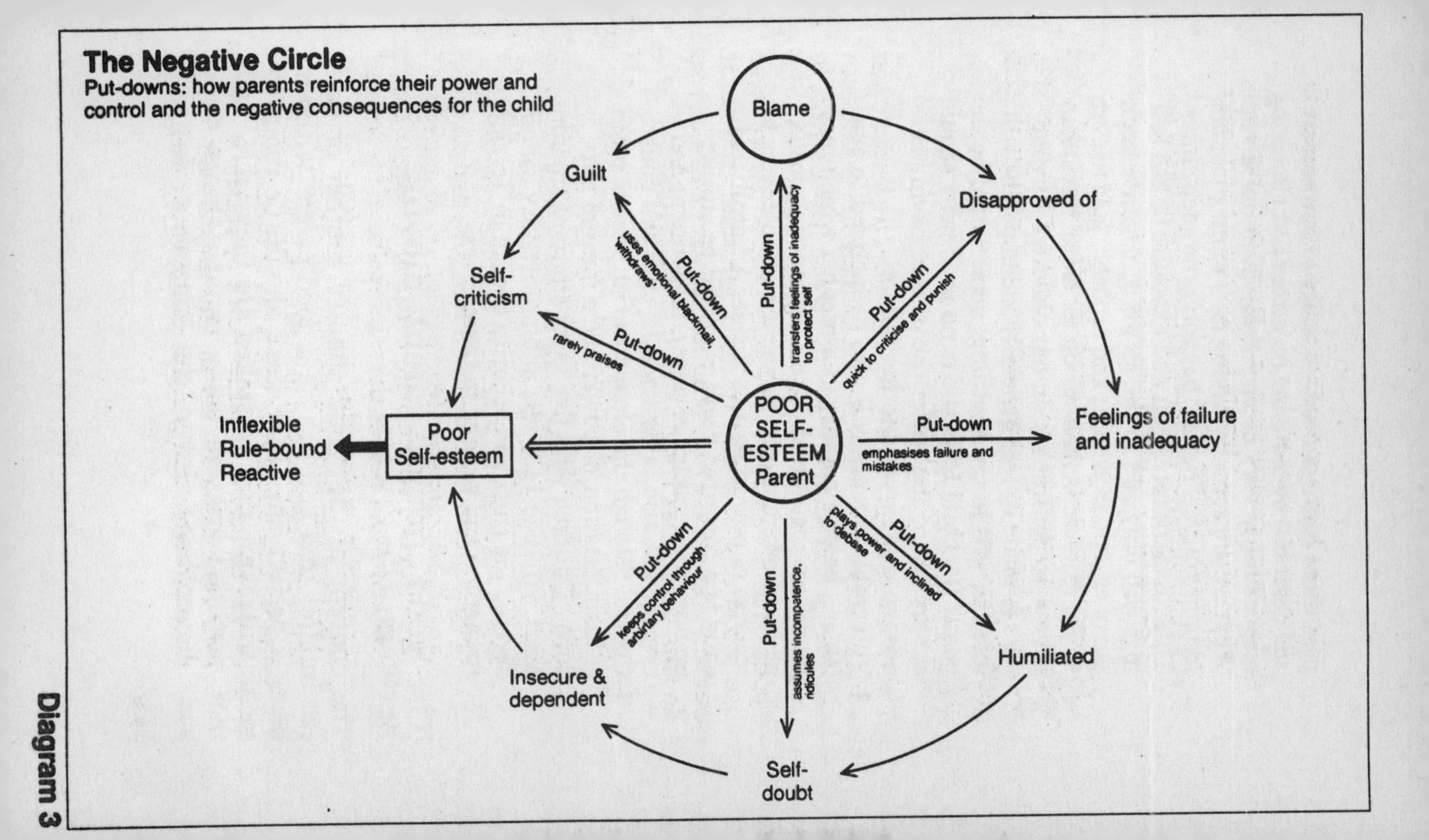
The Negative Circle
Put-downs: how parents reinforce their power and control and the negative consequences for the child
Blame
Guilt
Disapproved of
Self-criticism
Feelings of failure and inadequacy
Humiliated
Self-doubt
Insecure & dependent
Poor Self-esteem
Inflexible
Rule-bound
Reactive
POOR SELF-ESTEEM Parent
Put-down
transfers feelings of inadequacy to protect self
Put-down
quick to criticise and punish
Put-down
emphasises failure and mistakes
Put-down
plays power and inclined to debase
Put-down
assumes incompetence, ridicules
Put-down
keeps control through arbitrary behaviour
Put-down
rarely praises
Put-down
uses emotional blackmail, 'withdraws'
Diagram 3

pass these feelings over – usually to our nearest - and dearest – by focusing on errors and allocating responsibility very clearly *away from ourselves.* What we are actually saying is, *'I'm no good, and it makes me feel better that you're no good either.'* This further expression and exposure of bad feelings will only add to the swirling, negative cocktail of emotions present and probably lead to even worse reactive behaviour on all sides. But it can have a deeper impact on our children. Anyone who is made to feel generally incompetent will lose the will to try anything: what would be the point? If a child feels she is no good, why should she try again, and suffer the pain of having her nose rubbed in yet another failure?

- Vulnerable parents will also be inclined to **punish** and **behave harshly** in a manner which may **humiliate** their child. Overt demonstrations of physical or emotional power are often covers for feelings of powerlessness inside. A humiliated child is a cowering child who will be storing up not only feelings of anger, resentment and revenge but also layer upon layer of self-doubt.
- Control through the element of surprise is another manifestation of power and a form of put-down. Children who live in an arbitrary environment with constant fear and uncertainty cannot develop the trust and security needed to develop, strengthen and believe in themselves.

The 'good enough' parent: moving between the circles

The concept of the 'good enough' mother or parent implies that you can be a good parent without being a perfect one; that there should be room to make mistakes, that mistakes are inevitable; and that, provided you are doing enough things right and demonstrate love, the mistakes do not matter or do serious harm. It is an important, useful, and also a comforting idea which can reduce our destructive sense of guilt and help us to cope better.

However, when not fully understood, it can be exploited to justify and excuse behaviour which is neither justifiable nor excusable. It can be used to avoid trying to understand, change or take responsibility for our less attractive behaviour. *'I'll forget what I have just said or done, even though I know it was pretty nasty, because I know I love my kid really, so that's OK.'* But this kind of thought is just not good enough! Before we rest on our laurels in the comfort of believing that we have been 'good enough', and have provided a 'safety net' level of care, we need to be crystal clear about how good is 'good enough', and what it is we need to be good at.

What should be measured is love, care and commitment. And what matters is not whether *you think* you are giving these things, but whether *the child perceives* that he is receiving them. Love and care are *demonstrated* through commitment. You can say you love your child until you are blue in the face, but if you do not also demonstrate it so that he believes you, it will count for very little. Inevitably, then, the exact height of the hooks on which to attach this 'safety net', or hammock, of love and care through which you should not let your child fall, will be different in different cases.

If being a 'good enough' parent means demonstrating love and commitment most of the time, it will involve making your child feel good about himself and not putting him down. In practical terms, therefore, it means spending much of your time in the positive circle rather than the negative circle. It also means recognising quite quickly when you have strayed into the negative one, and knowing how to manage your behaviour while you are there so that you can move out again. For example:

- When you are feeling upset about something, at a low ebb, and get bad tempered, instead of blaming your child and making him feel bad, you can take responsibility for your mood. *'I've had an awful day and I'm in a foul mood. I'd steer clear of me for an hour if I were you!'* After this warning, if you do snap, the child will not take it personally.
- Instead of putting your child down and shrugging it off, because you think you are good enough, you can quite easily repair the damage and make reparation by doing or saying something which restores his self-esteem and faith in himself and your love for him. Implementing 'The Expertise' (see Chapter Five) and praising him, spending time with him, showing pride and interest in his skills, and thereby getting the warm glow of positive feedback from him about how much he values your time and commitment, are all techniques to use to switch across from the negative to the positive circle of behaviour which reinforces trust, respect, love and commitment.
- Try to improve your own self-image from time to time. Keeping on the positive track may require more than merely saying and doing the right thing for them from time to time.

Most of us move between the circles. We have good days and bad days. A '*not* good enough' parent is one who:

- strays *and stays* in the negative circle for prolonged periods of time;
- finds it hard to accept any measure of equality in the relationship;
- finds it hard to accept any responsibility for commitment;

- fails to demonstrate authority, only using the language and tactics of power which increase inequalities

Conclusion

Being a parent is, for most people, their greatest challenge. Children can give us our best moments, but they can also bring us face to face with our worst moments. Managing the emotional storms which are often unleashed, from our side as well as theirs, takes patience, a great deal of understanding, and even more skill.

'Positive parenting' is important. We now know that the quality and style of parenting can have a powerful effect on the future chances of a child – on his ability to learn, on his willingness to live within a structured framework, and on his chances of having sustained and fulfilled relationships. Having positive self-esteem is central to achieving these aims. Parents need to learn how to make children feel good about themselves. We need to improve our understanding of why we behave as we do. We need to develop skills to manage the changes, stresses and conflicts which characterise parenthood.

Good parenting is not intuitive and it is not learned overnight. 'Positive parenting' requires a new contract of commitment from everyone who cares about the quality of life for our children and the future of our society. With more support from government and the wider community to reduce the social and economic pressures on families and to spread good practice, parents will be better equipped to meet their first commitment, which has to be to their child.

Additional Reading

Bettelheim, Bruno *A Good Enough Parent*, Thames and Hudson, 1989
– *The Uses of Enchantment*, Penguin, 1979
Cleese, John and Skynner, Robin *Families and How to Survive Them*, Vermilion, 1993
Collins, Stephen *Step-Parents and their Children*, Souvenir Press, 1988
De'ath, Erica *Step-Parenting*, Family Doctor Publications, 1988
Elliott, Michele *Keeping Safe*, New English Library, 1986
Faber, Adele and Mazlish, Elaine *Siblings Without Rivalry*, New York: Avon Books, 1987
– *How to talk so Kids Will Listen and so Kids Will Talk*, New York: Avon Books, 1982
– *Liberated Parents/Liberated Children*, New York: Avon Books, 1975
Ginott, Haim *Between Parent and Child*, New York: Macmillan, 1965
Goldstein, Sol *Divorced Parenting*, Methuen, 1987
Hauk, Paul *Making Marriage Work*, Sheldon Press, 1981
– *How to Love and be Loved*, Sheldon Press, 1983
Hillman, Mayer Ed. Children, *Transport and the Quality of Life*, PSI Publishing, 1993
– *One False Move: A Study of Children's Independent Mobility*, PSI Publishing, 1990
Miller, Alice *The Drama of Being a Child*, Virago, 1987

Open University, The, Various study packs for parents offering guidance and understanding
Peiffer, Vera *How to Cope with Splitting Up*, Sheldon Press, 1991
Sokolov, Ivan and Hutton, Deborah *The Parents Book*, Thorsons, 1988
Steinem, Gloria *Revolution From Within: A Book of Self-Esteem*, Bloomsbury, 1992
Wells, Rosemary *Helping Children Cope with Divorce*, Sheldon Press, 1989
– *Helping Children Cope with Grief*, Sheldon Press, 1988

Useful Organisations

PROMOTING SELF-ESTEEM

Self-Esteem Network

32 Carisbrooke Road, London, E17 7EF

Co-ordinates the growing national interest in self-esteem and runs workshops and seminars on promoting self-esteem in policy and practice.

SUPPORT FOR PARENTS

Crysis

BMCry-sis, London, WC1B 3XX Tel: 0171 404 5011

Offers counselling advice if you feel your baby cries excessively.

Exploring Parenthood

4 Ivory Place, 20 Treadgold Street, London, W11 4BP Tel: 0171 221 4471/6681 (advice).

Workshops and discussion groups to explore the problems and pleasures of being a parent.

Family Welfare Association

501 Kingsland Road, London, E8 Tel: 0171 254 6251

Aims to challenge the causes of poverty and to help meet the needs of families and children living in poverty.

Gingerbread

16–17 Clerkenwell Close, London, EC1R 0AA TEL: 0171 336 8183

A network of local self-help groups for single parents.

Home Start UK

2 Salisbury Road, Leicester, LE1 7QR Tel: 0116 233 9955

Offers support, friendship and practical help to families under stress in their own homes.

Meet-a-Mum Association

Cornershore House, 14 Willis Road, Croydon, Surrey, CR0 4HS Tel: 0181 665 0537

Offers support and help for any mum who feels exhausted, isolated and in need of friendship. National network offering one-to-one and group support.

National Council for One-Parent Families

255 Kentish Town Road, London, NW5 Tel: 0171 267 1361

Provides a free information service for lone parents, training and consultancy services for lone parents and for employers and professionals who work with them. NCOPF also acts as a national voice for lone parents to government.

Newpin

Sutherland House, 35 Sutherland Square, London, SE17 3EE Tel: 0171 703 6326

Provides support, group-work, training and crèches to families at risk of abusing or being abused.

Parent Network

Winchester House, Kennington Park, 11 Cranmer Road, SW9 6EJ Tel: 0171 735 1214.

Practical and emotional support for parents. Also support and educational groups (known as Parent-Link).

Stepfamily

Chapel House, 18 Hatton Place, EC1N 8RU Tel: 0171 372 0844

Provides information, newsletters, support and counselling to members. There is a nationwide network of support groups. Counselling telephone line, 0171 372 support groups. Counselling telephone line, 00171 372 0846, is staffed by trained counsellors from 2-5 pm and 7-10pm every day.

PROTECTING CHILDREN'S INTERESTS

Child Poverty Action Group

1 Bath Street, London, EC1V 9PY Tel: 0171 253 3406

Promotes action for the relief, directly or indirectly, of poverty among children and families with children in the UK.

National Children's Bureau

8 Wakley Street, London, EC1V 7QE Tel: 0171 843 6000

Aims to identify and promote the interests of all children and to improve their status in a diverse society. Seeks to achieve this through research, policy development and the promotion of good practice in education, social work and health care.

NSPCC

42 Curtain Road, London, EC2A 3NH Tel: 0171 825 2500

Operates in England, Northern Ireland and Wales. See directory for local branches. NSPCC aims to prevent child abuse in all forms and to give practical help to families with children at risk.

HELP WITH RELATIONSHIP PROBLEMS

London Marriage Guidance

76a New Cavendish Street, London, W1M 7LB Tel: 0171 580 1087

Offers a marital and couple counselling service to Inner London and the London area.

Marriage Counselling, Scotland

105 Hanover Street, Edinburgh, EH2 1DG Tel: 0131 225 5006

As above, for Scotland.

Relate (Marriage Guidance)
Herbert Gray College, Little Church Street, Rugby, CV21 3AP Tel: 01788 573241
Provides a completely confidential counselling service for relationship problems of any kind. Local branches are listed in the telephone directory under Relate.

PLAY

For information on play schemes in your area, contact the town hall or your local library.

Fair Play for Children in Scotland
Unit 29, 6 Harmony Row, Glasgow, G51 3BA Tel: 0141-425 1140
Voluntary organisation to promote and encourage play opportunities for children. Runs workshops for play leaders and local communities on play opportunities e.g. traditional street games, flight etc.

Kidscape Children's Charity
152 Buckingham Palace Road, London, SW1W 9TR Tel: 0171-730 3300
Teaches children about personal safety and preventing abuse. Offers full teaching programmes, books for parents and children, videos, free information leaflets and posters. Also provides training in the use of its prevention and anti-bullying programmes.

National Play Information Centre
199 Knightsbridge, London SW7 1DE Tel: 0171 584 6464
Provides information about books and resources on play for children of all ages and local play facilities. Enquiries on all aspects of children's play welcome.

Woodcraft Folk
13 Ritherdon Road, London, SW17 8QE Tel: 0181 672 6031
An international organisation with no religious con-

nections which co-ordinates children's weekly mixed clubs for boys and girls, with an outdoor focus.

FAMILY AND CHILDREN'S LEGAL RIGHTS

Children's Legal Centre

20 Compton Terrace, London, N1 2UN Tel: 0171 359 6251

Advice line, 0171 559 6251, open 2-5pm daily.

Family Rights Group

18 Ashwin Street, London, E8 3DL Tel: 0171 923 2628

Advises parents, relatives or carers who have children in contact with social services departments or whose children are involved in child protection procedures.

PRE-SCHOOL EDUCATION

National Association for Gifted Children

Elder House, Milton Keynes, MK19 1LT Tel: 01908 677/8

Offers support to parents and professionals and runs enrichment clubs through local branches for able children to attend to help develop their potential. Pack for under-fives available.

Pre-School Learning Alliance

England" 61 Kings Cross Road, London, WC1X 9LN Tel: 0171 833 0991

Scotland: 14 Eliot Place, Glasgow, G3 8EP Tel: 0141 221 4148

Northern Ireland: Boucher Crescent, Boucher Road, Belfast BT12 6HU Tel: 01232662825

Wales: 2a Chester Street, Wrexham, Clwyd, LL18 8BD Tel: 01978 358 195

Promotes public interest in the value of play. Hundreds of voluntary area organisers and branches nationwide. Parents' role considered crucial and their involvement in the child's pre-school experience is encouraged

Telephone Help Lines:
Childline 0800 1111
Child Protection Help Line (NSPCC) 0800 800 500
Parentline 0268 757077

Index of Main Issues

Also by Elizabeth Hartley-Brewer and published by Vermilion –

Motivating Your Child

Tools and Tactics to Help Your Child Be A Self-Starter

We all dream of having children who get on with it and do well. When they don't, we fear the worst so we nag and push. But this approach can leave children feeling even less inspired.

In her new book Elizabeth Hartley-Brewer looks at what motivates people in business and sport and adapts these principles for parents and their children. Using a new model of motivation, she shows how, from the start, we can create a climate at home which fosters self-motivation and encourages self-managed achievement in a range of skills.

Other Positive Parenting Titles published by Vermilion –

Your Child's Symptoms Explained
Everything you need to know before you call the doctor

by David Haslam

This must-have handbook for every parent tells you how serious your child's symptoms are, what could be causing them, and whether or not to call in the doctor. Dr David Haslam helps parents to understand common children's symptoms and to answer such questions as: How can I tell if my child has a fever? What are the implications of a sore throat, coughing, vomiting, or constipation? What treatment – if any – is required? Organised by type of symptom, with a comprehensive index of ailments, this is an invaluable home reference book.

Home Birth

A comprehensive guide to planning childbirth at home

by Nicky Wesson

This book is a practical guide for the growing number of women who are considering having their babies delivered at home. It deals with the safety of mother and baby, parents' rights and the way to obtain a home birth. It also looks at the attitudes of family, friends and the medical establishment.

Childhood Development

by Dr Joan Gomez

In this fascinating and thorough investigation of the progression of a child's development from conception to pre-teens, Dr Joan Gomez explains clearly and concisely why what is normal development for one child is not necessarily standard for all.

The book contains a thorough assessment of the common milestones and influences on development from baby and toddlerhood to pre-adolescence. It includes useful reference charts for monitoring the development of your child including teething and sleep patterns and differences in growth patterns between boys and girls.